SCOTS-IRISH LINKS
1575–1725

PART FOUR

by
David Dobson

CLEARFIELD

Printed for
Clearfield Company by
Genealogical Publishing Co.
Baltimore, Maryland
2004

Reprinted for
Clearfield Company by
Genealogical Publishing Co.
Baltimore, Maryland
2006, 2007

ISBN-13: 978-0-8063-5256-5
ISBN-10: 0-8063-5256-6

Made in the United States of America

INTRODUCTION

The Plantation of Ulster by Scots in the seventeenth century is a well-established fact. Genealogists, however, require very specific reference material which is generally missing from the published accounts of the migration of up to 100,000 Scottish Lowlanders to northern Ireland at that time.

Part Four of *Scots-Irish Links, 1575-1725* attempts to identify some of these Scots settlers and is based mainly on contemporary primary source material found in Ireland and Scotland. A substantial number of the entries listed are based on documentary evidence held in the National Archives of Scotland in Edinburgh, especially rent rolls, estate papers, church records and port books.

Within a few generations, the descendants of these Ulster Scots emigrated in substantial numbers across the Atlantic where, as the Scotch-Irish, they made a major contribution to the settlement and development of Colonial America.

David Dobson
St Andrews, Scotland, 2004.

SCOTS-IRISH LINKS, 1575-1725.

[Part Four]

ABERCORN, Countess of, an undertaker in County Tyrone, with 2000 acres, 40 men, 24 swords, 36 pikes, 7 muskets, etc. [1641 Muster Roll of Ulster]

ABERCORN, Master of, an undertaker in County Cavan, with 2500 acres, 51 men, 39 swords, 10 pikes, 1 muskets, etc. [1641 Muster Roll of Ulster]

ACHESON, Sir ARCHIBALD, an undertaker in County Cavan, with 1000 acres, 20 men, 14 swords, 8 pikes, etc.; an undertaker in County Armagh, with 3000 acres, 56 men, 4 swords, 28 pikes, etc. [1641 Muster Roll of Ulster]

ACHESON, Sir GEORGE, in Carrickleane, parish of Kilclinoy, County Armagh, 1659. [C]

ACHESON, HENRY, was granted 1000 acres of Coolemalish in the precinct of Feus, County Armagh, on 26 April 1610. [TCD]

ACHESON, PATRICK, in Omagh, 1660-1670. [Hearth Money Rolls]

ADAIRE, ANDREW, in St John's town, Barony of Granard, County Longford, 1659. [C]

ADAIRE, ANDREW, in Tullagh, Tirrawley Barony, Killala parish, County Mayo. [BSD, 1636-1703]

ADAIRE, JAMES, a gentleman in the parish of Moylmey, Barony of Antrim, 1659. [C]

ADAIRE, WILLIAM, in Ballymenagh, Barony of Toome, County Antrim, 1659. [C]

ADAM, ARCHIBALD, in the Barony of Glenarm, 1650s, tenant of 30 acres in the parish of Kilwaghter, 1660s?. [NAS.GD154.512/525]

ADAM, JOHN, in the Barony of Glenarm, 1650s. [NAS.GD154.512]

ADAM, ROBERT, in the Barony of Glenarm, 1650s. [NAS.GD154.512]

AGNEW, ANDREW, in the Barony of Glenarm, 1650s, tenant in the parish of Kilwaghter, 1660s. [NAS.GD154.512/525]

AGNEW, Sir ANDREW, in the Barony of Glenarm, 1650s. [NAS.GD154.512]

AGNEW, ANDREW, a tenant in the parish of Kilwaghter, 1690. [NAS.GD154.525]

AGNEW, DAVID, merchant on the James of Belfast at Barbados in 1668. [ActsPCCol.#755]

AGNEW, EDMOND, tenant of 4 acres in the parish of Kilwaghter, 1660s. [NAS.GD154.525.2/2]

AGNEW, EDMOND GREEN, in the Barony of Glenarm, 1650s. [NAS.GD154.512]

AGNEW, GILBERT, tenant of 14 acres in Lelish, parish of Kilwaghter, 1690, 1692. [NAS.GD154.525/527/530]

AGNEW, Captain JOHN, 1654; in the Barony of Glenarm, 1650s, tenant in the parish of Kilwaghter, 1660s. [NAS.GD154.512/517/525]

AGNEW, JOHN, in the Barony of Glenarm, 1650s. [NAS.GD154.512]

AGNEW, KATHERINE, 1675. [NAS.RH15.91.60]

AGNEW, NIVEN, in County Antrim, 1658, husband of Elizabeth Porterfield. [NAS.GD154.275]

AGNEW, Sir PATRICK, OF LOCHNAW, leased the townlands of Lelies, Drumidonochie, Drumicho and Balliadedawn, in the Toche of Larne, from Sir Randal McDonell for 77 years on 29 April 1636. [NAS.GD154.505]

AGNEW, PATRICK, in Ballileill, had a lease of Ballikeill and part of the townland of Drumidonachie in Larne, from Sir Patrick Agnes and his son Andrew Agnew in 1636. [NAS.GD154.506]

AGNEW, PATRICK, tenant in Leales and Drumnicho, May 1645. [NAS.GD154.509]

AGNEW, PATRICK, tenant of 50 acres in the Barony of Glenarm, 1650s, tenant in the parish of Kilwaghter, 1660s. [NAS.GD154.512/515/525]

AGNEW, PATRICK, of Bushmills, 1657. [NAS.GD154.520]

AGNEW, PATRICK, in Ballikeill, Drumnedonachie, 1657, 1659. [NAS.GD154.519/521]

AGNEW, PATRICK, of Kilwaghter, 1665. [NAS.GD154.523/524]

AGNEW, PATRICK, of Kilwaghter in Ireland, was admitted as a burgess and guilds-brother of Ayr on 11 March 1675; appointed as rent collector in Kilwaghter by Sir Andrew Agnew of Lochnaw, 20 November 1693, bond dated 1 August 1695; receipt dated 7 August 1704. [ABR][NAS.GD154.531/533]

AGNEW, PATRICK, a tenant in the parish of Kilwaghter, 1690. [NAS.GD154.525]

AGNEW, PATRICK, tenant of 8 acres in Drumnadonochie, 1695. [NAS.GD154.532]

AGNEW, ROBERT, master of the <u>Ann of Belfast,</u> arrived in port Glasgow on 1 January 1682 from Belfast. [NAS.E72.19.5]

AGNEW, THOMAS, a pupil at Lord Donegall's school in Belfast, 1686. [NAS: Agnew of Lochnaw pp#D154/935]

AGNEW, WALTER, in the Barony of Glenarm, 1650s. [NAS.GD154.512]

AGNEW, ..., in the Barony of Belfast, 1659. [C]

AIKEN, ROBERT, son of the late Robert Aiken a clerk, a Protestant and proprietor of Druminevey, parish of Ray, Barony of Killmaccrenan, County Donegal, 1654. [CS]

AIKEN, ROBERT, a Protestant cleric in the parish of Clandehurka, 1654. [CS]

AIKEN, SAMUEL, servant to John Lennox in Londonderry, was admitted as a burgess and guilds-brother of Ayr on 3 September 1706. [ABR]

ALEXANDER, FERGUS, a member of the Presbytery of Bangor, 27 September 1649. [NAS.CH1/5/4/59]

ALEXANDER, JAMES, an undertaker in County Longford, 1621. [RPCS.XII.420]

ALEXANDER, WILLIAM, an undertaker in County Longford, 1621. [RPCS.XII.420]

ALEXANDER, WILLIAM, tenant of 30 acres in the parish of Kilwaghter, 1660s. [NAS.GD154.525.2/2]

ALGEO, ROBERT, agent for Sir William Hamilton of Eliston, in Londonderry, 1631. [NAS.E661.142]

ALGEO, ROBERT, a Catholic, son of the late Robert Algeo, parish of Leckpatrick, Barony of Strabane, County Tyrone, 1654. [CS]

ALGEO, ROBERT, a gentleman in Karrowkill and Rany, parish of Tully, Barony of Killmccrenan, County Donegal, 1659. [C]

ALISON, WILLIAM, in the Barony of Glenarm, 1650s, tenant in Kilwaghter parish, 1660s? [NAS.GD154.512/525]

ALLAN, JAMES, in the Barony of Glenarm, 1650s. [NAS.GD154.512]

ALLAN, JOHN, in Glasgow, was alleged to have supplied weapons to the rebels in Ireland, 1601. [RPCS.V.324]

ALLAN, ROBERT, a shipmaster of Belfast, 1726. [NAS.AC9.967]

ALLAN, WILLIAM, his wife and family, Protestant refugees in Scotland, formerly in the parish of Cumber, County Down, 1689. [RPCS.XIII.525]

ANDERSON, GEORGE, a merchant in Belfast, 1689, [RPCS.XIII.583]; was admitted as a burgess and guilds-brother of Ayr on 22 June 1697. [ABR]

ANDERSON, WILLIAM, a gentleman in Letterkenny town, parish of Conwall, Barony of Killmccrenan, County Donegal, 1659. [C]

ANDREW, JOHN, tenant of 30 acres in the Barony of Glenarm, 1650s. [NAS.GD154.512/515]

ANNANDALE, Earl of, an undertaker in County Donegal, with 10,000 acres, 143 men, 4 swords, etc. [1641 Muster Roll of Ulster]

ANNANDALE, JAMES, Earl of, a Protestant and leasee in the parishes of Killomard, of Enver, of Killoghtey, Killbegs, Killkare, Inshkeill, Templecron, Barony of Boylagh and Banoch, County Donegal, 1654. [CS]

ARBUCKLE, JAMES, a merchant in Belfast, 1689. [RPCS.XIII.583]

ARCHIBALD, JAMES, tenant of 15 acres in the Barony of Glenarm, 1650s. [NAS.GD154.512/515]

ARCHIBALD, JAMES, tenant of 37 acres in Drumadonachan, parish of Kilwaghter, 1690, 1693, 1695. [NAS.GD154.525/527/529/532]

ARCHIBALD, JOHN, in Kilwaghter, 1690. [NAS.GD154.527/1]

ARCHIBALD, widow, in Kilwaghter, 1690. [NAS.GD154.527/1]

ARMSTRONG, GEORGE, of Kinmount, a thief from the Borders, was captured in Ireland during 1679. [RPCS.VI.158]

ARMSTRONG, LANCE, a thief from the Borders, brother of Andrew Armstrong of Kirkton, was banished to Ireland on 10 June 1620. [RPCS.XII.288]

ARMSTRONG, THOMAS, a thief from the Scottish Borders, brother of Andrew Armstrong of Kirkton, was banished to Ireland on 10 June 1620, [RPCS.XII.288]; later apprehended in Ireland and returned to Scotland, where he was imprisoned in Dumfries Tolbooth in 1632. [RPCS.IV.496]

ARMSTRONG, ..., in the Barony of Antrim, 1659. [C]

ARMSTRONG, ..., in County Fermanagh, 1659. [C]

ARMSTRONG, the widow, 1675. [NAS.RH15.91.60]

ARSTALL, MARTIN, a Protestant and leasee in the parish of EnisMcSainte, Barony of Tirhugh, County Donegal, 1654. [CS]

ARTHUR, JAMES, in Kilwaghter, 1690. [NAS.GD154.527/1]

ASHLER, (?), JOHN, in the Barony of Glenarm, 1650s. [NAS.GD154.512]

ASHLER,(?), WILLIAM, in the Barony of Glenarm, 1650s. [NAS.GD154.512]

AUCHMUTY, ALEXANDER, granted the lands of Keylagh in the Barony of Tullaghcanco, County Cavan, 1610. [TCD]

AULD, GEORGE, tenant of 2 acres in the parish of Kilwaghter, 1660s. [NAS.GD154.525.2/2]

BACCON, ROBERT, in Artikillie, 1695 [NAS.RH15.91.49]

BAILLIE, Captain, 1694. [NAS.RH15.91.60]

BAILLIE, Captain JAMES, master of the <u>Mary of Belfast</u>, to Barbados by 1726. [NAS.AC9.967]

BAIRD, ROBERT, in Artikillie (?), 16... [NAS.RH15.91.49]

BALFOUR, Lord, an undertaker in County Fermanagh, with 5000 acres, 95 men, 37 swords, 11 pikes, etc. [1641 Muster Roll of Ulster]

BALFOUR, ..., in County Fermanagh, 1659. [C]

BALLOGH, JOHN, in Artikillie (?), 16... [NAS.RH15.91.49]

BARCLAY, HUGH, a gentleman in the parish of Lifford, Barony of Rapho, County Donegal, 1659. [C]

BARCLAY, ROBERT, a Protestant and leasee in the parish of Rapho, County Donegal, 1654. [CS]

BARCLAY, ROBERT, a Protestant cleric in the parish of Clogher, County Tyrone, 1654. [CS]

BARCLAY, WILLIAM, the elder, of Towie, was buried in Church of St Michael the Archangel, in Dublin, during 1675. [NAS.RH15/52/3]

BARCLAY, Captain WILLIAM, was buried in Church of St Michael the Archangel, in Dublin, during 1675. [NAS.RH15/52/3]

BARCLAY, WILLIAM, master of the <u>William of Hollywood</u> arrived in Port Glasgow on 21 December 1680 from Belfast. [NAS.E72.19.1]

BARNETT, JOHN, tenant of 30 acres in the Barony of Glenarm, 1650s. [NAS.GD154.512/515]

BARR, JOHN, leased the townland of Gorticaron, parish of Dunboe, County Londonderry, on 12 June 1655. [NAS.RH15.91.59]

BARR, WILLIAM, a tenant in Lisdrumbard, 1651.
[NAS.GD154.510]

BARR, WILLIAM, in the Barony of Glenarm, 1650s.
[NAS.GD154.512]

BAXTER, JOHN, a gentleman in Gortleg, parish of Conwall,
Barony of Killmccrenan, County Donegal, 1659. [C]

BEALIE, JOHN, son of William Bealie, in County Tyrone, 1657.
[NAS.GD154.274]

BELIONE, ADAM, leased 100 acres of Drumnicho for 1 year from
Andrew Agnew in May 1645. [NAS.GD154.509]

BELL, ALLAN, in Glasgow, was alleged to have supplied weapons
to the rebels in Ireland, 1601. [RPCS.V.324]

BELL, FERGUS, in the Barony of Glenarm, 1650s.
[NAS.GD154.512]

BELL, JOHN, 1694. [NAS.RH15.91.60]

BELL, ROBERT, in Knocklegane, Killcomen parish, County
Mayo. [BSD, 1636-1703]

BELL, THOMAS, leased the townland of Ballemoney, parish of
Dunboe, County Londonderry, on 4 September 1655.
[NAS.RH15.91.59]

BELL, ..., in the Barony of Belfast, 1659. [C]

BLACK, JOHN, a merchant in Belfast, bond 29 April 1678.
[Kirkcudbright Sheriff Court Records, deed #266]

BLACK, ..., in the Barony of Toome, County Antrim, 1659. [C]

BLAIR, ANDREW, tenant in Drumnicho, May 1645.
[NAS.GD154.509]

BLAIR, ANDREW, tenant of 20 acres in Lelish, parish of
Kilwaghter, 1690, 1693. [NAS.GD154.525/527/532]

BLAIR, BOYES, tenant of 6 acres in Barony of Glenarm, 1653. [NAS.GD154/515]

BLAIR, JAMES, son of Robert Blair the minister at Bangour and his wife Beatrice, daughter of Robert Hamilton, 1635. [RGS.IX.324]

BLAIR, JAMES, in the Barony of Glenarm, 1650s, tenant in Kilwaghter parish, 1660? [NAS.GD154.512/525]

BLAIR, JAMES, a tenant in Lisdrumbard, 1651. [NAS.GD154.510]

BLAIR, JAMES, a preacher of the Gospel, eldest son of Bryce Blair a merchant in Belfast, was admitted as a burgess and guilds-brother of Ayr on 19 November 1706. [ABR]

BLAIR, JOHN, tenant in Drumnadonachie, May 1645. [NAS.GD154.509]

BLAIR, JOHN, in the Barony of Glenarm, 1650s, tenant in Kilwaghter parish 1660s. [NAS.GD154.512/525]

BLAIR, JOHN, a tenant in Lisdrumbard, 1651. [NAS.GD154.510]

BLAIR, ROBERT, master of the ......of Coleraine at the port of Ayr on 3 May 1667. [NAS.E71.3.2]

BLAIR, ROBERT, leased the townland of Bellywolerikbeg, parish of Dunboe, County Londonderry, on 2 July 1655. [NAS.RH15.91.59]

BLAIR, SAMUEL, tenant of 3 acres in Drumadonachan, parish of Kilwaghter, 1690, 1692, 1695. [NAS.GD154.525/527/530/532]

BLAIR, WILLIAM, a passenger on the Speedwell of Glenarm at the port of Ayr on 27 July 1673. [NAS.E71.3.3]

BLAIR, ..., in the Barony of Antrim, 1659. [C]

BOLL, THOMAS, in the Barony of Glenarm, 1650s. [NAS.GD154.512]

BOLTON, HUGH, in Kilwaghter, 1690. [NAS.GD154.527/1]

BOLTON, JOHN, in Kilwaghter, 1690. [NAS.GD154.527/1]

BONE, ALEXANDER, 1694. [NAS.RH15.91.60]

BOSTON, ADAM, tenant of 66 acres in the Barony of Glenarm, 1650s, tenant in the parish of Kilwaghter, 1660s? [NAS.GD154.512/515/525]

BOSWELL, JOHN, in Carnecroy, Killmaine Barony, Templemore parish, County Mayo. [BSD, 1636-1703]

BOWMAN, ANDREW, 1694. [NAS.RH15.91.60]

BOYD, ADAM, of Bushmills, 16 October 1657. [NAS.GD154.519]

BOYD, ALEXANDER, master and merchant of the New John of Larne at Kirkcudbright harbour 16 November 1689. [NAS.E72.6.20]

BOYD, DAVID, a merchant in Dublin, was admitted as a burgess and guildsbrother of Ayr on 15 July 1717. [ABR]

BOYD, FRANCIS, a merchant in Portaferry, County Down, 1709. [NAS.GD25.Sec8/862]

BOYD, Major GEORGE, in County Antrim, subscribed to an obligation in favour of Sir George Montgomery of Skelmorlie, Ayrshire, on 12 July 1661. [NAS.GD3.2.51.24]

BOYD, HUGH, a merchant in Belfast, 1702. [NAS.GD154.532/533]

BOYD, JAMES, son of the late Bishop of Lismore, was a prisoner in Carrickfergus, Ireland, during 1654. [RSA#2/47]

BOYD, JAMES, a gentleman in Ballymore, on the island of Rathry, County Antrim, 1659. [C]

BOYD, JOHN, in Kilbryde, was alleged to have supplied weapons to the rebels in Ireland, 1601. [RPCS.V.324]

BOYD, JOHN, in the Barony of Glenarm, 1650s. [NAS.GD154.512]

BOYD, JOHN, in Moylmey, Barony of Antrim, 1659. [C]

BOYD, JOHN, a merchant in Belfast, 1690. [NAS.GD26.8.84]

BOYD, JOHN, born 1710, a surgeon, died 15 July 1776. [Ramoan g/s, County Antrim]

BOYD, ROBERT, in the Barony of Glenarm, 1650s. [NAS.GD154.512]

BOYD, ROBERT, from Ireland, in Dumfries by 19 June 1690. [NAS.CH2.537.15.1.34]

BOYD, THOMAS, in the Barony of Glenarm, 1650s, tenant in Kilwaghter parish 1660s? [NAS.GD154.512/525]

BOYD, THOMAS, a merchant in Wood Key Ward, Dublin, 1659. [C]

BOYD, ..., in the Barony of Toome, County Antrim, 1659. [C]

BRATTANE, JAMES, in Ireland around 1652. [Mouswald KSR, 15.2.1652]

BREDEN, THOMAS, 1694. [NAS.RH15.91.60]

BRISBANE, WILLIAM, a Protestant and a proprietor in the parish of Cappy, Barony of Strabane, County Tyrone, 1654, son and heir to William Brisbane deceased. [CS]

BROWN, HUGH, a merchant in Down, 1694. [NAS.RH15.91.60]

BROWN, JOHN, in the Barony of Glenarm, 1650s. [NAS.GD154.512]

BROWN, JOHN, leased the townland of Glasentarny, parish of Dunboe, County Londonderry, on 13 July 1655. [NAS.RH15.91.59]

BROWN, JOHN, a seaman of Belfast, to be released from Edinburgh or Canongate Tolbooth in July 1689. [RPCS.XIII.554]

BROWN, ROBERT, a Protestant and leasee in the parish of Rapho, County Donegal, 1654. [CS]

BROWN, ROBERT, tenant of 16 acres in Drumadonachan, parish of Kilwaghter, 1690, 1692. [NAS.GD154.525/530]

BROWN, WILLIAM, in the Barony of Glenarm, 1650s. [NAS.GD154.512]

BRUCE, ANDREW, son of Alexander Bruce of Wester Abden, and Agnes Calendar, daughter of George Calendar a minister in Clenarie, County Antrim, a marriage contract dated 2 February 1655. [NAS.GD6/1361]

BRUCE, ANTONY, born around 1603, settled in Ireland about 1650, a merchant traveller, took refuge in Scotland during 1690. [RPCS.XV.392]

BRUCE, MICHAEL, a fugitive minister from Ireland, accused of sedition and ordered to appear before the Privy Council, 23 June 1664. [RPCS.I.551]

BRUCE, MICHAEL a Presbyterian minister in northern Ireland, 1679. [RPCS.VI.657]

BRUCE, THOMAS, a gentleman in the parish of Taghboine, Barony of Rapho, County Donegal, 1659. [C]

BRUS, JOHN, in Omagh, 1660-1670. [Hearth Money Rolls]

BRYCE, JOHN, leased the townland of Glasentarny, parish of Dunboe, County Londonderry, on 13 July 1655. [NAS.RH15.91.59]

BRYCE, JOHN, a merchant from Dublin, in Ayr, Scotland, in 1690. [Ayr Burgh Charters & Records#90]

BUCHANAN, GEORGE, a Protestant and leasee in the parish of Rapho, County Donegal, 1654, [CS]; in Cullachybegg, parish of Rapho, 1659. [C]

BUCHANAN, ROBERT, a Protestant and leasee in the parishes of Ray and of Rapho, County Donegal, 1654. [CS]

BUCHANAN, WALTER, a gentleman in Letterkenny town, parish of Conwall, Barony of Killmccrenan, County Donegal, 1659. [C]

BURLEY, Lord, was granted lands of Legan in the Barony of Knocknyny, County Fermanagh, on 13 August 1610. [TCD]

BURNES, ..., in the Barony of Belfast, 1659. [C]

BURNETT, HENRY, a gentleman in the Barony of Rathdown, County Dublin, 1659. [C]

BURNSIDE, JOHN, a merchant in Silver Street, Londonderry, 1659. [C]

BURNSIDE, WILLIAM, master of the Vine of Londonderry, licensed as a privateer on 28 May 1689. [RPCS.XIII.387]

BURROWS, ALEXANDER, was murdered in Ireland by Robert Pilsworth during 1636. [RPCS.VI.279]

BUTLER, DAVID in Kilwaghter parish, 1692. [NAS.GD154/530]

CABON, ROBERT, tenant of 20 acres in Drumahoe, parish of Kilwaghter, 1690, 1692, 1695. [NAS.GD154.525/530/532]

CAIRNES, WILLIAM, a merchant in Dublin, was admitted as a burgess and guilds-brother of Ayr on 30 August 1686. [ABR]

CALDWELL, JAMES, in the Barony of Glenarm, 1650s. [NAS.GD154.512]

CALDWELL, JAMES, a merchant in Cork, was admitted as a burgess and guilds-brother of Ayr on 29 June 1719. [ABR]

CALDWELL, MOSES, 1694. [NAS.RH15.91.60]

CALDWELL, WILLIAM, in the Barony of Glenarm, 1650s. [NAS.GD154.512]

CALDWELL, WILLIAM, formerly keeper of the Register of Sasines for Ayrshire, then minister at Tamin, County Armagh, by 1673. [RPCS.III.13]

CALENDAR, AGNES, daughter of George Calendar minister in Clenarie, County Antrim, and Andrew Bruce, son of Alexander Bruce of Wester Abden, a marriage contract dated 2 February 1665. [NAS.RH9.7.43]

CALHOUNE, JAMES, in Corky, parish of Ray, Barony of Rapho, County Donegal, 1659. [C]

CALHOUNE, JOHN, a gentleman in Letterkenny town, parish of Conwall, Barony of Killmccrenan, County Donegal, 1659. [C]

CALHOUNE, PETER, a gentleman in Letterkenny town, parish of Conwall, Barony of Killmccrenan, County Donegal, 1659. [C]

CALHOUNE, WALTER, a gentleman in the parish of Leck, Barony of Rapho, County Donegal, 1659. [C]

CAMERON, ALEXANDER, minister in Kilbryde, then in Rasharkan, Ireland, 1683. [NAS.RS.Argyll.2/76]

CAMERON, ANNABELLA, daughter of Alexander Cameron, minister in Kilbryd then in Rasharkan, Ireland, 1715. [NAS.RS,Dunbarton#4/232]

CAMERON, JAMES, minister at Ballywalter (?), County Down, 1700. [NAS.GD154.533/6]

CAMERON, VIOLET, daughter of Alexander Cameron a minister in Kilbryd then in Rasharkan, Ireland, 1715, 1725. [NAS.RS,Dunbarton#4/232; 5/363]

CAMLIN, JOHN, 1668. [NAS.RH15.91.60]

CAMPBELL, ARCHIBALD, brother to the laird of Lawers, present at the Siege of Dunyvaig, pre 1625. [RPCS.I.201]

CAMPBELL, COLIN, of Balleherring, Ireland, and wife Marion Campbell, daughter of Colin Campbell of Carrick, marriage contract dated 29 September 1634 in Rosenekill, Ireland, and 18 April 1634 in Roseneath, Scotland. [NAS.RD {C&S}494]

CAMPBELL, COLIN, a Protestant and proprietor in the parish of Clandevadock, Barony of Killmacrennan, County Donegal, 1654. [CS]; there in 1659, [C]

CAMPBELL, DUGALL, minister of Knapdale, Argyll, Scotland, absent in Ireland during 1648. [RSA#1/118, 123]

CAMPBELL, ISABEL, in the Barony of Glenarm, 1650s. [NAS.GD154.512]

CAMPBELL, ISABEL, from Islay, Argyll, Scotland, to Insch, Derry, Ireland, in 1657. [RSA#2/144]

CAMPBELL, JANET, spouse of John Peblis of Pethirland, dwelling in the parish of Balliemoney, Ireland, also spouse of James Bryding, and daughter of Alexander Campbell minister at Stevenston, 1632. [NAS.RS.Ayr#5/327]

CAMPBELL, JOHN, of Easter Over Lednoch, Commissary of the Scots Army in Ireland, 1649. [NAS.RD {C&S}545/170]

CAMPBELL, JOHN, a gentleman in the parish of Clandevadocke, Barony of Killmccrenan, County Donegal, 1659. [C]

CAMPBELL, MICHAEL, 1694. [NAS.RH15.91.60]

CAMPBELL, PATRICK, a Protestant and proprietor in the parish of Clandevadock, Barony of Killmacrennan, County Donegal, 1654. [CS]; there in 1659. [C]

CAMPBELL, PATRICK, book-seller in Dublin, 1689. [RPCS.XIII.580]

CAMPBELL, ROBERT, a gentleman in the parish of Clandevadocke, County Donegal, 1659. [C]

CAMPBELL, ROBERT, in Londonderry, 31 April 1674.
[NAS.CH1/5/6/132]

CAMPBELL, ROBERT, a minister who fled from Ireland and
settled in the parish of Rosneath by 1691. [RPCS.XVI.107]

CAMPBELL, THOMAS, a gentleman in Drumcose, Barony of
Kenaght, County Londonderry, 1659. [C]

CAMPBELL, ..., in the Barony of Belfast, 1659. [C]

CAMPBELL, the widow, 1675. [NAS.RH15.91.60]

CAREMONT, JAMES, from Ireland, in Dumfries by 14
November 1689. [NAS.CH2.537.15.1.15]

CARMICHAEL, HEW, brother of John Carmichael of Redmyre,
an alleged thief who absconded from Falkirk to Ireland, but
returned in 1623. [RPCS.XIII.382]

CARNDERSE, JAMES, leased the townland of Gorticaron, parish
of Dunboe, County Londonderry, on 12 June 1655.
[NAS.RH15.91.59]

CARNOCHAN, ANDREW, 1694. [NAS.RH15.91.60]

CARRUTHERS, WILLIAM, from Ireland, in Dumfries by 9
January 1690. [NAS.CH2.537.15.1.24, 27]

CARSHILL, THOMAS, in the Barony of Glenarm, 1650s.
[NAS.GD154.512]

CARSWELL, JOHN, master of the John of Holywood arrived in
Kirkcudbright on 1 July 1690 from Ireland. [NAS.E72.6.20]

CASIER, ROBERT, a ropemaker in Ringsend, Dublin, was
admitted as a burgess and guilds-brother of Ayr on 12 June
1721. [ABR]

CASLAND, OLIVER, the sheriff of County Tyrone, 1689.
[RPCS.XIII.580]

CASTLESTEWART, Lord, a Protestant and proprietor in the parishes of Clunio, and of Donagh-Henry, County Tyrone, 1654. [CS]

CATHCART, ..., in County Fermanagh, 1659. [C]

CHAGARTIE, PATRICK, a Catholic priest from Ireland, in the Western Islands in 1631. [RPCS.IV.391]

CHALMER DAVID, senior, a merchant in Belfast, was admitted as a burgess and guilds-brother of Ayr on 4 July 1697. [ABR]

CHALMER, DAVID, junior, a merchant in Belfast, was admitted as a burgess and guilds-brother of Ayr on 5 October 1696. [ABR]

CHALMERS, JAMES, a merchant in Belfast, was admitted as a burgess and guilds-brother of Ayr on 11 May 1665. [ABR]

CHALMERS, JAMES, 1679. [NAS.RH15.91.60]

CHAMBERS, the widow, tenant of 30 acres in Drumahoe, parish of Kilwaghter, 1690, 1692. [NAS.GD154.525/530]

CHANCHER, ROBERT, servant of Patrick Agnew of Kilwachter in Ireland, was admitted as a burgess of Ayr on 11 March 1675. [ABR]

CHARTERS, WILLIAM, from Ireland, in Dumfries by 26 December 1689. [NAS.CH2.537.15.1.22]

CHIRIS, ROBERT, in Artikillie, 1695 [NAS.RH15.91.49]

CHREISTY, JAMES, a servant to Colin Maxwell, MD, in Londonderry, was admitted as a burgess and guilds-brother of Ayr on 3 September 1706. [ABR]

CLANIE, WILLIAM, servant to Reverend Archibald Hamilton in Bangor, Ireland, was admitted as a burgess and guilds-brother of Ayr on 28 September 1675. [ABR]

CLARK, JAMES, a candlemaker, 1694. [NAS.RH15.91.60]

CLARK, the widow, 1694. [NAS.RH15.91.60]

CLELAND, HUGH, 1674, 1694. [NAS.RH15.91.60]

CLELAND, JAMES, late provost of Bangour, County Down, was admitted as a burgess of Irvine, Ayrshire, on 13 May 1667. [Irvine Council Book]

CLELAND, THOMAS, 1694. [NAS.RH15.91.60]

CLEPHANE, JAMES, was granted 2000 acres in Newton and in Lislop in the precinct of Strabane, County Tyrone, on 28 April 1610. [TCD]

CLERK, ROBERT, from Ayr, was plundered of his goods while bound for the west of Ireland in 1616. [NAS.RH9.17.32/2]

CLUGSTON, ROBERT, in Newton, Ireland, 10 January 1645. [NAS.CH1/5/4/27]

COBHAM, THOMAS, a Presbyterian minister in northern Ireland 1679, [RPCS.VI.657]; a minister who fled with his family to Scotland, settled in Penningham by 1691. [RPCS.XVI.33]

COCKBURN, WILLIAM, the younger of that Ilk, arrived in Scotland from Ireland in 1691. [RPCS.XVI.221]

COLDEN, ALEXANDER, a minister who fled from Ireland in April 1689 and settled in the parish of Duns. [RPCS.XVI.141]

COLEMAN, JAMES, a merchant in Dublin, was admitted as a burgess and guilds-brother of Ayr on 4 July 1715. [ABR]

COLQUHOUN, Sir JOHN, a Protestant and a leasee in the parish of Ray, County Donegal, 1654. [CS]

COLQUHOUN, ..., of Luss, undertaker in County Donegal, with 1000 acres, 9 men, 6 swords, 4 pikes, etc. [1641 Muster Roll of Ulster]

COLVILLE, Lord JAMES, born 1604, eldest son of Robert Colville and Christina Bruce, moved to Ireland in 1640, granted lands of Bally McLaughlin, County Kilkenny, in

1649, died in 1654, buried in Trinity Church, Dublin. [SP.II.558]

COLVILL, JAMES, in Antrim, 1659. [C]

COLVILL, ROBERT, in Galgorme, Barony of Toome, 1659. [C]

COMBE, MATHEW, justice of the peace for County Antrim, 1675. [NAS.RH9.17.103]

COMBLIN, ALEXANDER, 1694. [NAS.RH15.91.60]

COMBLIN, GILBERT, and his children, moved from Ireland, to Dumfries, by 7 November 1689. [NAS.CH2.537.15.1.14]

COMYN, JAMES, a gentleman in Tallaghgore, parish of Bellemone, County Antrim, 1659. [C]

CONN, JOHN, tenant of 15 acres in the Barony of Glenarm, 1650s. [NAS.GD154.512/515]

CONYNGHAM, ANNA, heir to Sir James Conyngham, a Protestant, leasee in the parish of Taboyne, County Donegal, 1654, *'Anna Conyngham holdeth ye pmises by patent granted in the name of Jas Conyngham of Balliachan for the use of the sd heretrix of Sr James Conyngham of Glengormocke'.* [CS]

CONYNGHAM, FRANCES, widow of Robert Conyngham, a Protestant, a leasee in the parish of Taboyne, County Donegal, 1654, *'ye relict of Mr Robt. Coningham holdeth ye two Qrs. Of Coricamen and Drumlocher by purchase from Robt. Coningham, son of Alexr. Coningham who held the same in freehold by Patent'..* [CS]

CONYNGHAM, GEORGE, *'holdeth ye Qr. land of Drumay as heire to his father who held ye same in freehold from Sr. James Conyngham deceased'.* 1654. [CS]

CONYNGHAM, GEORGE, who was at the Battle of Worcester, a leasee in the parish of Rapho, County Donegal, 1654. [CS]

CONYNGHAM, JAMES, a Protestant and leasee in the parish of Lecke, County Donegal, 1654. [CS]

CONYNGHAM, Sir JOHN, undertaker in County Donegal, with 2000 acres, 124 men, 70 swords, 38 pikes, 3 muskets, etc. [1641 Muster Roll of Ulster]

CONYNGHAM, Sir JOHN, deceased, a Protestant, leasee in the parish of Taboyne, County Donegal, 1654. [CS]

CONYNGHAM, MARGARET, *'ye relict of Andrew Coningham holdeth a ballibo of the pmises called Ballihasky wth a house and tenemt and six acres of land in Colmiltraine and a garden plot in the Bukehill neare adjacent.* 1654. [CS]

CONYNGHAM, PATRICK, *'the sonne of Alexr. Coningham holdeth ye Qr. Land of Letrum in freehold .... Also [he] and his mother Jenet Barton holdeth ye Qr. Land of Portlough by purchase in fee farme from Sir James Conyngham'.* 1654.[CS]

CONYNGHAM, Lieutenant Colonel WILLIAM, heir of Sir John Conyngham, leasee in the parish of Taboyne, County Donegal, 1654. [CS]

CONYNGHAM, WILLIAM, brother of George Conyngham, leasees in the parish of Rapho, County Donegal, 1654. [CS]

CONYNGHAM, Lady, undertaker in County Donegal, with 2000 acres, 66 men, 33 swords, 10 pikes, etc. [1641 Muster Roll of Ulster]

COOKE, JAMES, in Carrikins, parish of Tabrone, County Donegal, 1654. [CS]

COOPER, JOHN, 1694. [NAS.RH15.91.60]

COOSH, JOHN, in the Barony of Glenarm, 1650s. [NAS.GD154.512]

COPRAN, THOMAS, a merchant from Dublin, in Edinburgh on 21 May 1586. [RPCS.IV.72]

CORBETT, ALLAN, a merchant in Belfast, 1683.
[NAS.RH15.91.60]

CORLAT, JOHN, a prisoner brought from Ireland to Scotland in
1690. [RPCS.XV.278]

CORNER, THOMAS, in the Barony of Glenarm, 1650s.
[NAS.GD154.512]

COTTER, ROBERT, 1694. [NAS.RH15.91.60]

COULTHARDE, JAMES, in the townland of Clony, 1690.
[NAS.RH15.91.59]

COUPAR, THOMAS, 1694. [NAS.RH15.91.60]

COUTARD, JANE, a servant, 1694. [NAS.RH15.91.60]

COWAN,......., in the Barony of Belfast, County Antrim, 1659. [C]

CRAFFORD, MATHEW, a gentleman in Bellibune, parish of
Donoghmore, Barony of Rapho, County Donegal, 1659. [C]

CRAGG, JAMES, was granted part of Magerietrim in the precinct
of Feus, County Armagh, in September 1610. [TCD]

CRAGG, Sir JAMES, undertaker in County Cavan, with 2000
acres, 54 men, 16 swords, 15 pikes, 6 muskets, etc. [1641
Muster Roll of Ulster]

CRAIG, JAMES, was granted 1000 acres of Mcgherientrim in the
precinct of Feus, County Armagh, on 26 April 1610. [TCD]

CRAIG, JOHN, a merchant in Diamond Street, Londonderry,
1659. [C]

CRAIG, MARGARET, born 1681, wife of Francis Scott of
Templepatrick, died 5 May 1741. [Donegore g/s, County
Antrim]

CRAIG,......., in the Barony of Belfast, County Antrim, 1659. [C]

CRAWFORD, JAMES, in the Barony of Glenarm, 1650s. [NAS.GD154.512]

CRAWFORD, JAMES, master of the brigantine Batchelor of Belfast, was admitted as a burgess and guilds-brother of Ayr on 22 June 1725. [ABR]

CRAWFORD, JOHN, a gentleman on Moylmey, Barony of Antrim, 1659. [C]

CRAWFORD, MALCOLM, a gentleman in Killduff, parish of Ballynycloghy, Barony of Conagh, County Limerick, 1659. [C]

CRAWFORD, MATTHEW, brother of the laird of Lesnoreis, returned to Scotland under a legal protection to settle a dispute between his brother and Gabriel Porterfield of Hapland in 1631. [RPCS.IV.327]

CRAWFORD, Captain PATRICK, sent to Carrickfergus, Ireland, with 200 soldiers in June 1608. [RPCS.VIII.511]

CRAWFORD, ROBERT, in Cullaghy, Drumra parish, Omagh, 1660-1670. [Hearth Money Rolls]

CRAWFORD, ..., in the Barony of Antrim, 1659. [C]

CRICHTON, ALEXANDER, a Protestant and proprietor in the parish of Dissertireagh, Barony of Dungannon, County Tyrone, 1654. [CS]

CRICHTON, Sir ROBERT, or **MURRAY**, owner of the Baronyies of Boillach and Bannoch in Ireland, 1684. [RPCS.VIII.326]

CRICHTON, ROBERT, a merchant traveller, from Loch Larne to Saltcoats, Scotland, in 1686. [RPCS.XII.379]

CRICHTON, THOMAS, agent of Lord Aubigny, William Dunbar, and others in County Cavan, 1610. [TCD]

CRIGHTON, JAMES, a gentleman in the parish of Killagtie, Barony of Boylagh and Banagh, County Donegal, 1659. [C]

CRUICKSHANK, JOHN, the minister of Rapho, was admitted as a burgess and guilds-brother of Ayr on 14 June 1658, through the right of his wife Elizabeth, eldest daughter of John Birnie. [ABR]

CRUICKSHANK, JOHN, a fugitive minister from Ireland, accused of sedition and ordered to appear before the Privy Council, 23 June 1664. [RPCS.I.551]

CRUMEY, JOHN, in Artikillie, 1695 [NAS.RH15.91.49]

CUNNINGHAM, ALEXANDER, was granted part of Moynargan in the precinct of Boylaghe, County Donegal, on 9 September 1610. [TCD]

CUNNINGHAM, ALEXANDER, a Protestant, in the parish of Clandevadock, Barony of Killmaccrenan, County Donegal, 1654. [CS]

CUNNINGHAM, ALEXANDER, a gentleman in Letterkenny town, parish of Conwall, Barony of Killmccrenan, County Donegal, 1659. [C]

CUNNINGHAM, ALEXANDER, a gentleman in Beliara, parish of Killabegs, County Donegal, 1659. [C]

CUNNINGHAM, ANDREW, a gentleman in Beliara, parish of Killabegs, County Donegal, 1659. [C]

CUNNINGHAM, CUTHBERT, was granted part of Dromay in the Barony of Portloghe, County Donegal, on 6 September 1610. [TCD]

CUNNINGHAM, GEORGE, a gentleman in Tamnitullen, parish of Inver, Barony of Boylagh and Banagh, County Donegal, 1659. [C]

CUNNINGHAM, Sir JAMES, was granted lands of Dacastroose and Portloghe in the Barony of Rapho, County Donegal, on 4 September 1610. [TCD]

CUNNINGHAM, JAMES, was granted lands of Moyeghe in the precinct of Portloghe, County Donegal, on 4 September 1610. [TCD]

CUNNINGHAM, JAMES, leasee in Gallen Barony, Killasser parish, County Mayo. [BSD, 1636-1703]

CUNNINGHAM, JAMES, undertaker in County Donegal, with 1000 acres, 59 men, 31 swords, 10 pikes, etc. [1641 Muster Roll of Ulster]

CUNNINGHAM, JAMES, a Protestant, leasee in the parish of Ray, County Donegal, 1654. [CS]

CUNNINGHAM, JAMES, in Belliaghan, parish of Ray, Barony of Rapho, County Donegal, 1659. [C]

CUNNINGHAM, JAMES, son of Alexander Cunningham, a gentleman in Letterkenny town, parish of Conwall, Barony of Killmccrenan, County Donegal, 1659. [C]

CUNNINGHAM, JOHN, was granted Donbuy in the precinct of Portlogh, Barony of Raphoe, County Donegal, 4 September 1610. [TCD]

CUNNINGHAM, JOHN, in the Barony of Glenarm, 1650s. [NAS.GD154.512]

CUNNINGHAM, JOHN, son of James Cunningham, in Belliaghan, parish of Ray, Barony of Rapho, County Donegal, 1659. [C]

CUNNINGHAM, JOHN, a merchant from Sligo now in Ayr, was admitted as a burgess and guilds-brother of Ayr on 30 July 1690. [ABR]

CUNNINGHAM, JOHN, a Presbyterian minister in northern Ireland, 1679. [RPCS.VI.657]

CUNNINGHAM, PETER, leased the townland of Bellywolerikbeg, parish of Dunboe, County Londonderry, on 2 July 1655. [NAS.RH15.91.59]

CUNNINGHAM, WILLIAM, in Articlare, County Londonderry, 1635. [NAS.RH15.91.61]

CUNNINGHAM, WILLIAM, a Protestant gentleman in Ballendrum, parish of Artrea, Barony of Coleraine, County Londonderry, 1654. [CS]

CUNNINGHAM, WILLIAM, a gentleman in Tamnitullen, parish of Inver, Barony of Boylagh and Banagh, County Donegal, 1659. [C]

CUNNINGHAM, WILLIAM, a gentleman in Plaister, parish of Taghboine, Barony of Rapho, County Donegal, 1659. [C]

CUNNINGHAM, WILLIAM, in Monfad, parish of Taghboine, Barony of Rapho, County Donegal, 1659. [C]

CUNNINGHAM, Lieutenant Colonel WILLIAM, in Ballymcegan, parish of Lorha, County Tipperary, 1659. [C]

CUNNINGHAM, …., in the Barony of Toome, County Antrim, 1659. [C]

CUNYNGHAM, JOHN, a Protestant and a proprietor in Balligay the parish of Tully, County Donegal, 1654. [CS]; there in 1659, [C]

CUNYNGHAM, JOHN, a Protestant gentleman in the parish of Conwall, Barony of Killmaccrenan, County Donegal, 1654. [CS]

CURRIE, GEORGE, an undertaker in County Longford, 1621. [RPCS.XII.420]

CUTHBERT, ROBERT, 1694. [NAS.RH15.91.60]

DALRYMPLE, CHARLES, 1702. [NAS.GD154.532]

DALYELL, THOMAS, an undertaker in County Longford, 1621. [RPCS.XII.420]

DAVIDSON, ROWIE, a thief who had fled to Ireland but had returned, to be sought for in Carrick, Ayrshire, during 1628. [RPCS.II.444]

DAVIDSON, WILLIAM, in Dalincover, son of Rowie Davidson , a thief who had fled to Ireland but had returned, to be sought for in Carrick, Ayrshire, during 1628. [RPCS.II.444]

DAVISON, JOHN, master of the Swan of Belfast, arrived in Dumfries in 168- from Bordeaux. [NAS.E72.6.25]

DAVISON, JOHN, 1694. [NAS.RH15.91.60]

DAWSON, JOHN, 1674. [NAS.RH15.91.60]

DENNISTON, JAMES, merchant of the Antelope of Glasgow in Tyrconnel, 1608. [RPCS.III.205]

DENNY, JOHN, a merchant in Pump Street, Londonderry, 1659. [C]

DICK, GEORGE, in Newton, Ireland, 10 January 1645. [NAS.CH1/5/4/27]

DICK, JAMES, a Protestant and leasee in the parish of Rapho, County Donegal, 1654. [CS]

DICKISON, THOMAS, 1694. [NAS.RH15.91.60]

DICKSON, RICHARD, a minister in Dunbarton, sentenced to be sent to Ayr then banished to Ireland on 30 July 1624, [RPCS.XIII.586, 624]

DICKSON, WILLIAM, 1694. [NAS.RH15.91.60]

DICKY, MATHEW, 1668. [NAS.RH15.91.60]

DINSMURE, JOHN, leased the townland of Drumnaguille, parish of Kelleve, County Londonderry, on 8 Augusty 1655. [NAS.RH15.91.59]

DISART, HUGH, in the Barony of Glenarm, 1650s. [NAS.GD154.512]

DOBIE, JOHN, 1694. [NAS.RH15.91.60]

DOCK, JAMES, in Ireland, serviced as heir to John Dock, smith burgess of Ayr, on 22 August 1654. [NAS.Retours]

DOGHIRTY, JOHN, a servant to Charles Norman in Londonderry, was admitted as a burgess and guilds-brother of Ayr on 3 September 1706. [ABR]

DOICK, ALEXANDER, master of the <u>Providence of Coleraine,</u> arrived in Ayr from Virginia via Londonderry in 1685. [NAS.E72.3.16]; skipper in Coleraine, was admitted as a burgess and guilds-brother of Ayr on 14 December 1687. [ABR]

DONALD, JAMES, in the Barony of Glenarm, 1650s, tenant of 10 acres in the parish of Kilwaghter, 1660s. [NAS.GD154.512/525]

DONALDSON, JAMES, a gentleman in Glenclives and Stradhill, parish of Tegmacrewa, County Antrim, 1659. [C]

DONALDSON, JOHN, in the Barony of Glenarm, 1650s, 1659. [NAS.GD154.512/522]; in Glenarm, parish of Tegmacrewa, County Antrim, 1659. [C]

DONALDSON, ..., in the Barony of Belfast, County Antrim, 1659. [C]

DORAGH, WILLIAM, a Protestant cleric in the parish of Derrygloran, Barony of Dungannon, County Tyrone, 1654. [CS]

DOUGAN, DAVID, 1694. [NAS.RH15.91.60]

DOUGAN, JOHN, of Bellywalter, County Down, a soldier, to return from Scotland to Ireland in 1689. [RPCS.XIII.425]

DOUGLAS, ALEXANDER, brother of late John Douglas of Howden, to Ireland in 1609. [RPCS.VIII.598]

DOUGLAS, ANDREW, born in Glasgow, settled at Coleraine around 1679, master of the <u>Phoenix of Coleraine</u>, was licensed as a privateer on 29 May 1689. [RPCS.XIII.389]

DOUGLAS, Sir JAMES, was granted 2000 acres in the precinct of Feus, County Armagh, on 26 April 1610. [TCD]

DOUGLAS, JAMES, a gentleman in the parish of Atherdee, County Louth, 1659. [C]

DOUGLAS, JAMES, in Lisburn, County Antrim, 1690. [NAS.GD26.9.271]

DOUGLAS, JOHN, of Howden, brother of Alexander Douglas, a soldier who fought for Queen Elizabeth in Ireland, settled there and died before 1609. [RPCS.VIII.598]

DOUGLAS, Mrs, a widow, in the Barony of Glenarm, 1650s. [NAS.GD154.512]

DOULL, DAVID, a tailor, 1694. [NAS.RH15.91.60]

DRAIN, JOHN, in the Barony of Glenarm, 1650s, tenant in the parish of Kilwaghter, 1660s [NAS.GD154.512/525]

DRUMMOND, Sir JOHN, of Borland, was granted 1000 acres in Ballimagnegh in the precinct of Strabane, County Tyrone, on 28 April 1610. [TCD]

DRUMMOND, THOMAS, a minister in the parish of Aghneish, Barony of Killmacrennan, County Donegal, 1654. [CS]

DRUMMOND, WILLIAM, an undertaker in County Longford, 1621. [RPCS.XII.420]

DRUMMOND, ..., an undertaker in County Tyrone, with 1000 acres, 15 men, 15 swords, 1 pikes, etc. [1641 Muster Roll of Ulster]

DRYSDAILL, JOHN, a member of the Presbytery of Bangor, 27 September 1649. [NAS.CH1/5/4/59]

DUN, GEORGE, 1694. [NAS.RH15.91.60]

DUNBAR, ALEXANDER, was granted part of Kilkeran in the precinct of Boylaghe, County Donegal, on 9 September 1610. [TCD]

DUNBAR, DAVID, in Kerucastle, parish of Auchnish, Barony of Killmccrenan, County Donegal, 1659. [C]

DUNBAR, GEORGE, a minister in Ayr, banished to Ireland on 30 July 1624, [RPCS.XII.586, 624]

DUNBAR, Sir JOHN, an undertaker in County Fermanagh, with 1000 acres, 10 men, 10 swords, 5 pikes, 4 muskets, etc. [1641 Muster Roll of Ulster]

DUNBAR, MARGARET, from Ireland, in Dumfries by 5 June 1690. [NAS.CH2.537.15.1.34]

DUNCAN, JAMES, master of the James of Glenarm from Ayr to Belfast in January 1691. [NAS.E72.3.27]

DUNDAS, Captain ALEXANDER, tenant in Listonbaird, May 1645. [NAS.GD154.509]

DUNDAS, Mrs, a widow, tenant of 3 acres in the parish of Kilwaghter, 1660s. [NAS.GD154.525.2/2]

DUNLOP, ADAM, a Protestant, in the parish of Clandevadock, Barony of Killmacrennan, County Donegal, 1654. [CS]

DUNLOP, ALEXANDER, tenant in Drumnicho, May 1645; tenant of 66 acres in the Barony of Glenarm, 1650s, tenant in the parish of Kilwaghter, 1660s. [NAS.GD154.509/512/515/525]

DUNLOP, ALEXANDER, in the Barony of Glenarm, 1650s. [NAS.GD154.512]

DUNLOP, ANDREW, a merchant in Dublin, was admitted as a burgess and guilds-brother of Ayr on 6 March 1723. [ABR]

DUNLOP, BRICE, a gentleman in Kircony, parish of Ramoan, County Antrim, 1659. [C]

DUNLOP, PATRICK, a minister who fled from Ireland in 1689, settled in Minigaff, Wigtownshire, by 1691. [RPCS.XVI.609]

DUNN, MARGARET, in Artikillie (?), 16… [NAS.RH15.91.49]

ECCLES, HUGH, a merchant in Belfast, a bond dated 29 April 1678. [Kirkcudbright Sheriff Court Records, deed #266]

ECLIS, GILBERT, late a merchant in Carrickfergus, was admitted as a burgess of Ayr on 1 January 1650. [ABR]

EDINSON, ARCHIBALD, in the Barony of Glenarm, 1650s. [NAS.GD154.512]

EDMINSTON, ARCHIBALD, husband of Ann Erskine, in the parish of Erregoll-Keirog, Barony of Clogher, County Tyrone, dead by 1654. [CS]

EDMOND, DANIEL, a merchant traveller in Ireland, with his wife Jean and children, from Dunlewar, County Liew (?), via Loch Larne to Saltcoats, Scotland, in 1686. [RPCS,XII.379]

EDMOND, JOHN, in the Barony of Glenarm, 1650s. [NAS.GD154.512]

EDMONDSTON, WILLIAM, a Protestant, in Eary, parish of Belliclogg, Barony of Dungannon, County Tyrone, 1654. [CS]

EDMONSTON, ARCHIBALD, on Broad Island, Barony of Belfast, County Antrim, 1659. [C]

EDMONSTON, JOHN, a gentleman in Broad Island, Barony of Belfast, County Antrim, 1659. [C]

EDWARDS, JAMES, master of the bark <u>Elizabeth of Larne,</u> from Port Glasgow to Belfast on 23 February 1681. [NAS.E72.19.2]

ELLIOT, JOHN, a prisoner brought from Ireland to Scotland in 1690. [RPCS.XV.278]

ELLIOT,. …, in County Fermanagh, 1659. [C]

ERSKINE, ANN, widow of Archibald Edmonston, a Protestant and proprietor in the Manor of Favour Royal, parish of Erregoll Keirog, Barony of Clogher, County Tyrone, 1654. [CS]

ERSKINE, ARCHIBALD, died in 1641, son of Sir James Erskine of Clogher, County Tyrone, father of Thomas, died in 1640s, Mary and Anne – alive in the Barony of Clogher in 1675. [NAS.RH9.17.103]

ERSKINE, CHARLES, son of Archibald Erskine, alive in County Tyrone 1675. [NAS.RH9.17.103]

ERSKINE, Sir JAMES, of Tullibody, and his spouse Dame Marie Erskine, around 1635. [NAS.RH9.17.103]

ERSKINE, Sir JAMES, of Ogher, County Tyrone, who died around 1635. father of Archibald and James. [NAS.RH9.17.103]

ERSKINE, Sir JAMES, an undertaker in County Tyrone, with 3000 acres, 138 men, 58 swords, 27 pikes, 3 muskets, etc. [1641 Muster Roll of Ulster]

ERSKINE, JAMES, a Protestant and a proprietor in the parish of Clogher, County Tyrone, 1654. [CS]

ERSKINE, JAMES, in Bogay, parish of Aghanunshen, County Donegal, 1659. [C]

ERSKINE, JAMES, son of Archibald Erskine, alive in County Tyrone 1675. [NAS.RH9.17.103]

ERSKINE, MARY, a Protestant and proprietor in the Manor of Favour Royal, parish of Erregoll Keirog, Barony of Clogher, County Tyrone, 1654. [CS]

ERWIN, WILLIAM, 1668. [NAS.RH15.91.60]

ERWIN, WILLIAM, 1694. [NAS.RH15.91.60]

ESLER, JAMES, tenant of 22 acres in Belliderdawn, 1695. [NAS.GD124.532]

ESPIE, JOHN, 1675. [NAS.RH15.91.60]

EUART, WILLIAM, merchant on the James of Donaghadie at Kirkcudbright on 8 September 1673. [NAS.E72.6.2]

EVANSTON, JOHN, 1694. [NAS.RH15.91.60]

EWAN, JOHN, *'claims the quarter land of Gortree by deed of purchase from Alex Coningham freeholder thereof'*, Parish of Taboyne, County Donegal, 1654. [CS]

EWING, ALEXANDER, a gentleman in Letterkenny town, parish of Conwall, Barony of Killmccrenan, County Donegal, 1659. [C]

EWING, ROBERT, a Protestant and proprietor in the parish of Conwall, County Donegal, 1654. [CS]

FAIRBAIRN, JOHN, a passenger on the Catherine of Larne at the port of Ayr on 20 August 1673. [NAS.E71.3.3]

FAIRIE, JAMES, in Kilbride, was alleged to have supplied weapons to the rebels in Ireland, 1601. [RPCS.V.324]

FAIRES, JOHN, 1694. [NAS.RH15.91.60]

FENTON, WILLIAM, a witness in Glenarm, 19 November 1651. [NAS.GD154.510]

FENTON, WILLIAM, a gentleman in Bellyhankett, parish of Carncastle, County Antrim, 1659. [C]

FERGUSON, ALEXANDER, a Presbyterian minister in northern Ireland, 1679. [RPCS.VI.657]

FERGUSON, ANNE, 1694. [NAS.RH15.91.60]

FERGUSON, JANE, relict of Captain William Barclay, was buried in Church of St Michael the Archangel, in Dublin, during 1675. [NAS.RH15/52/3]

FERGUSON, M., 1694. [NAS.RH15.91.60]

FERGUSON, ..., in the Barony of Antrim, 1659. [C]

FIDDIS, HUGH, 1694. [NAS.RH15.91.60]

FINDLEY, JOHN, a tenant in Lisdrumbard, 1651.
[NAS.GD154.510]

FINLAY, HANS, 1694. [NAS.RH15.91.60]

FINNIE, JOHN, leased the townland of Dingonie, parish of
Dunboe, County Londonderry, on 30 June 1655.
[NAS.RH15.91.59]

FISHER, DOROTHY, born 1679, died 18 April 1696.
[Templepark g/s, County Antrim]

FISHER, EDWARD, from Ireland, in Dumfries by 17 April 1690.
[NAS.CH2.537.15.1.29]

FISHER, JAMES, a merchant in Butcher's Gate, Londonderry,
1659. [C]

FISHER, JOHN, master of the bark Marie of Coleraine, from Port
Glasgow to Coleraine on 4 January 1681. [NAS.E72.19.2]

FISHER, MARGARET, 1674. [NAS.RH15.91.60]

FISHER, WILLIAM, in Artikillie (?), 16... [NAS.RH15.91.49]

FITZSYMONS, NORIS, in Down, County Down, 1683.
[NAS.GD10.830]

FLEMING, JOHN, in the parish of Mevagh, Barony of
Killmccrenan, County Donegal, 1659. [C]

FLEMING, ROBERT, a gentleman in Collidue, parish of Movill,
Barony of Enishowen, County Donegal, 1659. [C]

FORBES, Sir ARTHUR, in Lisnagree, Athlone Barony, Camma
parish, County Roscommon. [BSD, 1636-1703]

FORBES, JAMES, an undertaker in County Longford, 1621.
[RPCS.XII.420]

FORBES, JAMES, a merchant in Dublin, around 1722.
[NAS.CC8.8.89/539]

FORBES, ROBERT, an undertaker in County Longford, 1621.
[RPCS.XII.420]

FOREST, GEORGE, a seaman of Belfast, to be released from
Edinburgh or Canongate Tolbooth in July 1689.
[RPCS.XIII.554]

FORREST, JAMES, and his wife Catherine Sheirer, leased the
townland of Lusock, Clarneity and Ardidillan, parish of
Dunboe, County Londonderry, on 20 August 1655.
[NAS.RH15.91.59]

FORRETT, JAMES, an undertaker in County Longford, 1621.
[RPCS.XII.420]

FORSTER, JOHN, Justice of the Peace, recorder of Dublin, 1712.
[NAS.GD10.498]

FORSYTH, HUGH, in Artikillie (?), 16... [NAS.RH15.91.49]

FORSYTH, JAMES, a minister in Kirkpatrick, father of James and
Robert, who was banished to Ireland in 1638. [RPCS.I.215]

FORSYTH, JOHN, in Artikillie, 1695 [NAS.RH15.91.49]

FULLERTON, Mr, in County Fermanagh, with 120 acres, 2 men,
2 swords, etc. [1641 Muster Roll of Ulster]

FULTON, JOHN, a Protestant and leasee in the parish of Rapho,
County Donegal, 1654. [CS]

FULTON, THOMAS, a merchant in Wood Key Ward, Dublin,
1659. [C]

FULTON, THOMAS, near Newton of Limnivaddy, March 1672.
[NAS.CH1/5/6/126]

FULTON, ..., in the Barony of Belfast, County Antrim, 1659. [C]

GALBRAITH, HUMPHREY, claims land of Gortmore, parish of Ray, County Donegal, formerly held by his late brother James, 1654. [CS]

GALBRAITH, JAMES, a late leasee in the parish of Ray, County Donegal, 1654. [CS]

GALBRAITH, ROBERT, a leasee in the parish of Ray, Barony of Rapho, County Donegal, 1654, brother of Humphrey and James. [CS]; there in 1659. [C]

GALBREATH, JOHN, a tenant in Kilwaghter, 1692. [NAS.GD154.530]

GALE, Mr, a Protestant, late of the parish of Taboyne, County Donegal, 1654. [CS]

GALT, WILLIAM, 1694. [NAS.RH15.91.60]

GEDDES, JANE, 1694. [NAS.RH15.91.60]

GEMMILL, DAVID, member of the Presbytery of Bangor, 27 September 1649. [NAS.CH1/5/4/59]

GETTY, JAMES, rent collector in Kilwaghter, 1692. [NAS.GD154.530]

GIBB, JAMES, undertaker in County Longford, 1621. [RPCS.XII.420]

GIBB, RORY, in the Barony of Glenarm, 1650s. [NAS.GD154.512]

GIBONY, ALEXANDER, 1694. [NAS.RH15.91.60]

GIBONY, JAMES, 1668. [NAS.RH15.91.60]

GILCHRIST, THOMAS, a gentleman in Ballydonothie, parish of Camline, County Antrim, 1659. [C]

GILL, JOHN, in Artikillie (?), 16... [NAS.RH15.91.49]

GILLIES, JAMES, 1705. [NAS.GD154.532/533]

GIVAN, JOHN, in Omagh, 1660-1670. [Hearth Money Rolls]

GLASGOW, JAMES, in the Barony of Glenarm, 1650s. [NAS.GD154.512/525]

GLASGOW, JAMES, master of the James of Donaghadie at the port of Ayr on 26 August 1667; master of the James of Belfast at the port of Ayr on 13 October 1673. [NAS.E71.3.2/3]

GLASGOW, JOHN, passenger on the Venture of Glenarm at the port of Ayr on 30 October 1673. [NAS.E71.3.3]

GLASGOW, JOHN, witness, Kilwaghter, 1691. [NAS.GD154.528/1]

GLASS, JOHN, a Protestant and leasee in the parish of Rapho, County Donegal, 1654. [CS]

GLENDENNING, ROBERT, an undertaker in County Longford, 1621. [RPCS.XII.420]

GLENN, GEORGE, in Artikillie (?), 16... [NAS.RH15.91.49]

GLENN, GEORGE, in Artikillie, 1695 [NAS.RH15.91.49]

GOODLATT, JOHN, in the parish of Killamen, Barony of Dungannon, County Tyrone, dead by 1654. [CS]

GOODLATT, JOHN, a Protestant, claimed land in the parish of Donaghkiddy, Barony of Strabane, inherited by his wife Euphame from her first husband James Hamilton, 1654. [CS]

GOODLATT, ROBERT, in the parish of Killamen, Barony of Dungannon, County Tyrone, dead by 1654. [CS]

GORDON, ALEXANDER, a Presbyterian minister in northern Ireland, 1679. [RPCS.VI.657]

GORDON, ALEXANDER, 1694. [NAS.RH15.91.60]

GORDON, GEORGE, a gentleman in Ballelagh, parish of Calfachterney, County Antrim, 1659. [C]

GORDON, JAMES, the minister at Comber, was admitted as a burgess and guilds-brother of Ayr on 8 July 1656, through the right of his wife Elizabeth, eldest daughter of Robert Gordon the late Provost of Ayr. [ABR]; a Presbyterian minister in northern Ireland, 1679. [RPCS.VI.657]

GORDON, ROBERT, an undertaker in County Longford, 1621. [RPCS.XII.420]

GORM, DONALD, in Ireland, 1595. [CSPS.XII.15]

GRAHAM, Major ARTHUR, storekeeper at Enniskillen, County Fermanagh, 1667. [NAS.RH15.91.61]

GRAHAM, JAMES, of Gartur, married Elizabeth, daughter of Captain Philip Wilkieson in Balnahinch, Ireland, there in August 1714. [NAS.CC8.Process of Divorce, 16 December 1726]

GRAHAM, JOHN, a gentleman in Kilbreny, parish of Carrick, Barony of Shelmaleer, County Wexford, 1659. [C]

GRAHAM, KIRSTIE, of County Down, a soldier, to return from Scotland to Ireland in 1689. [RPCS.XIII.425]

GRAHAM, RICHARD, of Mullachbreck, County Ardmagh, a soldier, to return from Scotland to Ireland in 1689. [RPCS.XIII.425]

GRAHAM, WILLIAM, in Dublin, 1630. [NAS.GD22.V.1]

GRAHAM, Lieutenant, from County Fermanagh, with 200 acres, 8 men, 8 swords, 3 pikes, 2 muskets, etc. [1641 Muster Roll of Ulster]

GRAHAM, ..., in the Barony of Antrim, 1659. [C]

GRAHAM, ..., in the Barony of Belfast, County Antrim, 1659. [C]

GRAHAM, ..., in County Fermanagh, 1659. [C]

GRAHAM, Captain, in Newtown, Barony of Forth, County Catherlagh, 1659. [C]

GRANT, JAMES, a rebel, escaped from Edinburgh Castle on 13 October 1632 and headed for Ireland where his daughter lived. [RPCS.IV.544/578]

GRANT, PATRICK, a merchant in Waterford, 1659. [C]

GRAY, JOHN, a fisher in Glasgow, was alleged to have supplied weapons to the rebels in Ireland, 1601. [RPCS.V.324]

GRAY, J., member of the Presbytery of Bangor, 27 September 1649. [NAS.CH1/5/4/59]

GREAME, Sir GEORGE, granted 1000 acres in the Barony of Tullaghah, 1610. [TCD]

GREAME, Sir RICHARD, granted 1000 acres in the Barony of Tullaghah, 1610. [TCD]

GREEN, SAMUEL, 1694. [NAS.RH15.91.60]

GREENSHIELDS, JAMES, a minister, late curate of Tynan in the Diocese of Armagh, imprisoned in Edinburgh Tolbooth, 1709. [NAS.CH8.194]

GREG, JAMES, a merchant in Donaghadie in 1674. [NAS.RH15.91.60]

GREG, NICHOLAS, a miller and sub-tenant of Andrew Stewart, Lord Ochiltree, 1622. [NLI.MS8014/viii]

GREGORY, WILLIAM, of Londonderry. 7 February 1719. [Inveraray Sheriff Court Book, Vol.#VI]

GREIG, JOHN, a gentleman in the parish of Killagtie, Barony of Boylagh and Banagh, County Donegal, 1659. [C]

GREIG, ROBERT, in Artikillie (?), 16... [NAS.RH15.91.49]

GREIG, WILLIAM, in the Barony of Glenarm, 1650s. [NAS.GD154.512]

GREIR, GILBERT, from County Down, a soldier, to return from Scotland to Ireland in 1689. [RPCS.XIII.425]

GREIR, ROBERT, of Ballany, County Down, a soldier, to return from Scotland to Ireland in 1689. [RPCS.XIII.425]

GREIR, ROBERT, from Ords, County Down, a soldier, to return from Scotland to Ireland in 1689. [RPCS.XIII.425]

GREY, HUGH, a merchant in Dublin, was admitted as a burgess and guilds-brother of Ayr on 13 August 1713. [ABR]

GRIFFIN, NICHOLAS, in Coleraine, leased the farmlands of Killivittie, Knocknocher, and Bellibughtbegg, parish of Dunboe, County Londonderry, on 14 February 1655. [NAS.RH15.91.59]

GRIME, ISAAC, in Artikillie, 1695 [NAS.RH15.91.49]

GRIME, NATHANIEL, in Artikillie, 1695 [NAS.RH15.91.49]

GUTHRY, ALEXANDER, a Protestant and leasee in the parish of Ray, County Donegal, pre 1654. [CS]

GUTHRY, FRANCIS, a Protestant and a leasee in the parishes of Rapho, and of Inshkeill, County Donegal, 1654. [CS]

HAIG, JAMES, was granted part of Tirenemeriertagh in the precinct of Strabane, County Tyrone, on 8 September 1610. [TCD]

HALL, ALEXANDER, a gentleman in Ridbay, parish of Lays, County Antrim, 1659. [C]

HALL, RICHARD, master of 'the lytill bark', a document with links to Londonderry, no date but after 1613. [NAS.RH9.17.32/1]

HALL, ROBERT, a Protestant and freeholder of Ballifadden, Manor of Blissingburn, Parish of Clogher, Barony of Clogher, County Tyrone, 1654. [CS]

HAMIL, JOHN, in Irvine, was alleged to have supplied weapons to the rebels in Ireland, 1601. [RPCS.V.324]

HAMILTON, Captain ALEXANDER, born 1613, second son of Alexander Hamilton of Innerwick, Scotland, sixth brother of James, Lord Viscount Clanboy, husband of Mary, the eldest daughter of William Reading, parents of Patrick, Mary, and Elizabeth, died 1648. [Clandeboye Chapel g/s]

HAMILTON, Sir ALEXANDER, was granted lands in the Barony of Loghtree, County Cavan, 25 August 1610. [TCD]

HAMILTON, ALEXANDER, 1675. [NAS.RH15.91.60]

HAMILTON, ANDREW, a Protestant, landowner in the parishes of Rapho and of Donoghmore, County Donegal, 1654, *'the aforesaid Andrew Hamilton Esqr. Holdeth ye pmises as lawfull heire to sd. Jon. Wilson and Capn. Andrew Wilson uncles to ye sd Andrew Hamilton'.* [CS]

HAMILTON, ANDREW, a Protestant, leasee in the parishes of Donnoghmore and Rapho, County Donegal, 1654, which were inherited from his uncles Sir John Wilson and Andrew Wilson. [CS]

HAMILTON, ANDREW, a Protestant cleric of the parishes of Kilskirry and Maghericross, Barony of Omagh, County Tyrone, 1654. [CS]

HAMILTON, ARCHIBALD, sometime of Bearford then in Ireland, 1622. [RPCS.XII.746]

HAMILTON, ARCHIBALD, an undertaker in County Tyrone, with 1000 acres, 25 men, 21 swords, 5 pikes, 2 muskets, etc. [1641 Muster Roll of Ulster]

HAMILTON, ARCHIBALD, a Protestant and proprietor in Ballegallie, parish of Erregoll Keirog, Barony of Clogher, County Tyrone, 1654. [CS]

HAMILTON, ARCHIBALD, a leasee in the parish of Dromore, Barony of Omagh, County Tyrone, 1654. [CS]

HAMILTON, ARCHIBALD, minister of Bangor in Ireland, was admitted as a burgess and guilds-brother of Ayr on 28 September 1675. [ABR]; a Presbyterian minister in northern Ireland, 1679. [RPCS.VI.657]

HAMILTON, ARCHIBALD, a merchant in Belfast, was admitted as a burgess and guilds-brother of Ayr on 29 June 1719. [ABR]

HAMILTON, CHARLES, a Protestant and proprietor in the parishes of Conwall, of Gartan, and of Aghenunshen, County Donegal, 1654. [CS]

HAMILTON, CLAUD, was granted 1000 acres of Edeneaghe in the precinct of Feus, County Armagh, on 26 April 1610, and part of Edeneaghe in the Barony of Feus, County Armagh, on 4 September 1610. [TCD]

HAMILTON, CLAUD, an undertaker in County Longford, 1621. [RPCS.XII.420]

HAMILTON, Sir FRANCIS, an undertaker in County Cavan, with 3000 acres, 113 men, 24 swords, 25 pikes, 6 muskets, etc. [1641 Muster Roll of Ulster]

HAMILTON, Captain FRANCIS, a gentleman in Killmure, parish of Rapho, Barony of Rapho, County Donegal, 1659. [C]

HAMILTON, Sir FRANCIS, of Castle Kelly, Ireland, 24 July 1663. [NAS.RS.Berwick#1/119]

HAMILTON, FRANCIS, a gentleman in Monalan, Barony of the Lower Feus, County Armagh, 1659. [C]

HAMILTON, Sir FREDERICK, in Tirrawley Barony, Killala parish, County Mayo. [BSD, 1636-1703]

HAMILTON. Lieutenant GAVEN, 1694. [NAS.RH15.91.60]

HAMILTON, Sir GEORGE, of Greenlaw, resident in Strabane by 1620. [EUL.Laing.MS2/5][NLI.MS8014/ix]

HAMILTON, Sir GEORGE, an undertaker in County Tyrone, with 2500 acres, 54 men, 50 swords, 8 pikes, etc. [1641 Muster Roll of Ulster]

HAMILTON, Sir GEORGE, of Downelonge, a Catholic and a proprietor in the parish of Donoghkiddy, Barony of Strabane, County Tyrone, 1654. [CS]

HAMILTON, GUSTAVUS, in the parish of Lifford, Barony of Rapho, County Donegal, 1659. [C]

HAMILTON, HANS, of Cullgarne, gentleman, 1675. [NAS.RH9.17.103]

HAMILTON, HUGH, of Lisdevin, in the parish of Donoghkiddy, a Protestant, heir to his brother and father in the lands of Loghennease, parish of Leckpatrick, and in the parish of Donoghkiddy, Barony of Strabane, County Tyrone, 1654. [CS]

HAMILTON, HUGH, the elder of Drommanie, a Protestant and a proprietor in the parish of Donoghkiddy, Barony of Strabane, 1654. [CS]

HAMILTON, HUGH, of Moneygabin, born 1669, son of John Hamilton, and grandson of James Hamilton of Cloughcopphow, died 26 March 1748. [Ballymoney g/s, County Antrim]

HAMILTON, HUGH, from County Armagh, a soldier, to return from Scotland to Ireland in 1689. [RPCS.XIII.425]

HAMILTON, HUGH, 1694. [NAS.RH15.91.60]

HAMILTON, JAMES, in Krukbin, 1612. [NAS.RH15.91.59]

HAMILTON, JAMES, of Ballychemagry, County Tyrone, 1619. [NAS.RD1.301]

HAMILTON, JAMES, in County Tyrone before 1641. [NAS.RH9.17.103]

HAMILTON, JAMES, of Balligallie, a Justice of the Peace in County Tyrone, 1636. [NAS.GD10.743]

HAMILTON, JAMES, fought under the Duke of Hamilton, arrived after the Articles of Inniskillin, proprietor in the parishes of Tully, and of Mevagh, County Donegal, dead by 1654. [CS]

HAMILTON, JAMES, of Roskrea, son of Sir George Hamilton the elder of Roskrea, a Catholic and a proprietor in the parishes of Ardstragh, and of Leckpatrick, Barony of Strabane, County Tyrone, 1654. [CS]

HAMILTON, Lord JAMES, Barony of Strabane, a Catholic and a proprietor in the parishes of Ardstragh, of Camos and of Urney, Barony of Strabane, County Tyrone, 1654, son of Lord Claude Hamilton. [CS]

HAMILTON, JAMES, a gentleman in the Lyne of Mounteredy, Barony of Toome, County Antrim, 1659. [C]

HAMILTON, JAMES, a gentleman in Tallaghgore, parish of Bellemone, County Antrim, 1659. [C]

HAMILTON, JAMES, a gentleman in Fentraugh, parish of Killibegs, County Donegal, 1659. [C]

HAMILTON, JAMES, a merchant in Londonderry, 1664. [RPCS.I.487]

HAMILTON, JAMES, a merchant in Strabane, and master of the Beattie of Glasgow from Glasgow to Londonderry in 1689. [RPCS.XIV.51]

HAMILTON, JAMES, of Ords, County Down, a soldier, to return from Scotland to Ireland in 1689. [RPCS.XIII.425]

HAMILTON, JAMES, master of the <u>Resolution of Strangford</u> from Kirkcudbright to Ireland on 27 May 1689. [NAS.E72.6.20]

HAMILTON, JOHN, agent for Sir Claud Hamilton in the Barony of Tulachonchoe, 1610. [TCD]

HAMILTON, JOHN, an undertaker in County Cavan, with 1000 acres, 44 men, 10 swords, 3 pikes, 1 muskets, etc.; an undertaker in County Armagh, with 2500 acres, 113 men, 53 swords, 42 pikes, 2 muskets, etc. [1641 Muster Roll of Ulster]

HAMILTON, JOHN, a Protestant, claimed Moyagh, parish of Donaghkiddy,Barony of Strabane, as heir to his father John Hamilton, 1654. [CS]

HAMILTON, JOHN, in Cavan, parish of Donoghmore, Barony of Rapho, County Donegal, 1659. [C]

HAMILTON, JOHN, a gentleman in Shanon and Drumleer, parish of Donoghmore, Barony of Rapho, County Donegal, 1659. [C]

HAMILTON, JOHN, late of Clochcurr, Ireland, 1677. [GBR;20.1.1677]

HAMILTON, JOHN, a minister at Newton, Ireland, and by 1690 in Cramond, Scotland. [RPCS.XV.227]

HAMILTON, JOHN, 1694. [NAS.RH15.91.60]

HAMILTON, JOHN, a merchant in Belfast, was admitted as a burgess and guilds-brother of Ayr on 4 July 1697. [ABR]

HAMILTON, ROBERT, of Stonehouse, was granted 2000 acres in Ulster on 6 June 1609. [RPCS.VIII.586]

HAMILTON, ROBERT, was granted lands of Drumra, in the Barony of Maghereboye, County Fermanagh, on 4 September 1610. [TCD]

HAMILTON, ROBERT, a Protestant and leasee in the parish of Rapho, County Donegal, 1654. [CS]

HAMILTON, ROBERT, a Protestant, in Carrowcley, parish of
Urney, Barony of Strabane, County Tyrone, 1654. [CS]

HAMILTON, ROBERT, a gentleman in the parish of
Donoghmore, Barony of Rapho, County Donegal, 1659. [C]

HAMILTON, ROBERT, late minister of Ballabrae, now in
Killead, County Antrim, 1668. [NAS.GD109.1714]

HAMILTON, ROBERT, of Belliferris, merchant in Killileach,
County Down, fled to Scotland and died there in March 1689.
[RPCS.XIII.448]

HAMILTON, WILLIAM, the Provost of Strabane, 1620.
[NLI.MS8014/viii]

HAMILTON, Sir WILLIAM, an undertaker in County Tyrone,
with 2750 acres, 43 men, 42 swords, 22 pikes, etc. [1641
Muster Roll of Ulster]

HAMILTON, Sir WILLIAM, of Elyston, a Protestant and
proprietor in the parishes of Bodony and of Donoghkiddy,
Barony of Strabane, County Tyrone, 1654. [CS]

HAMILTON, WILLIAM, in County Tyrone, with 1000 acres, 14
men. [1641 Muster Roll of Ulster]

HAMILTON, WILLIAM, in Omagh, 1660-1670. [Hearth Money
Rolls]

HAMILTON, WILLIAM, of Killeach, Ireland, was admitted as a
burgess and guilds-brother of Ayr on 25 September 1699.
[ABR]

HAMILTON, WILLIAM, in Gallen Barony, Meelick parish,
County Mayo. [BSD, 1603-1703]

HAMILTON, WILLIAM, a seaman from Belfast, was killed at the
taking of Carrickfergus, husband of Barbara McDonald,
father of three children, pre 1690. [RPCS.XV.227]

HAMILTON, WILLIAM, of Killiragh, County Down, signed a deed of factory in favour of Archibald Hamilton of Killiragh, 1712. [NAS.GD25.SEC8/900]

HAMILTON, Mrs, a widow, an undertaker in County Cavan, with 1000 acres, 5 men, 5 swords, 3 pikes, etc.; an undertaker in County Fermanagh, with 1500 acres, 24 men, 22 swords, and 14 pikes. [1641 Muster Roll of Ulster]

HANNA, PATRICK, an undertaker in County Longford, 1621. [RPCS.XII.420]

HANNEY, WILLIAM, servant to Patrick Hanney in Wigtonshire, alleged armed assault, fled to Ireland in September 1630. [RPCS.IV.94]

HANNY, WILLIAM, a gentleman in Lisnegatt, parish of Kilclinoy, County Armagh, 1659. [C]

HARRIS, WALTER, in Dublin, 1689. [NAS.GD26.8.16]

HARSLIE, JOHN, in Artikillie, 1695 [NAS.RH15.91.49]

HARVEY, JOHN, a minister who fled from Ireland in April 1689, settled in Lochmaben parish. [RPCS.XVI.3]

HARVIE, ROBERT, a gentleman in Toberdornan, parish of Ballywillin, 1659. [C]

HAY, JOHN, minister in Renfrew, deposed in 1648, then a preacher in Donegal, father of Andrew Hay. [RPCS.I.342]

HENDERSON, ALEXANDER, a Protestant in the parish of Conwall, Barony of Killmaccrenan, County Donegal, 1654. [CS]

HENDERSON, GAVIN, from Hetland Hill, Mouswald parish, Dumfries-shire, a merchant traveller in Ireland around 1652. [Mouswald KSR, 1.2.1652]

HENDERSON, JOHN, a passenger on the Venture of Glenarm at the port of Ayr on 30 October 1673. [NAS.E71.3.3]

HENDRY, JOHN, possibly a burgess of Renfrew, settled in Killilooch, Ireland, as a fish merchant by 1637. [Dumbarton Burgh Records, 11.12.1637]

HENRY, ANDREW, in Artikillie, 1695. [NAS.RH15.91.49]

HENRY, HUGH, in Artikillie, 1695 [NAS.RH15.91.49]

HENRY, ROBERT, in Artikillie, 1695 [NAS.RH15.91.49]

HEPBURN, DAVID, master of the William and Joan of Belfast in the port of Greenock in August 1679, bound from there with passengers via Dublin for Accomack, Virginia. [NAS.RD3.48.513]

HEPBURN, Sir ROBERT, was granted 1500 acres of Ocauragan in the precinct of Mountjoy, County Tyrone, on 9 April 1610. [TCD]

HEPBURN, WILLIAM, in Bishop Gate Street, Londonderry, 1659. [C]

HERON, JOHN, was granted part of Donoghcoran in the Barony of Onealan, County Armagh, on 4 September 1610. [TCD]

HERON, NINIAN, an undertaker in County Longford, 1621. [RPCS.XII.420]

HERRON, THOMAS, 1694. [NAS.RH15.91.60]

HESLIP, RICHARD, 1694. [NAS.RH15.91.60]

HILL, M., 1694. [NAS.RH15.91.60]

HILLOUS, WILLIAM, 1694. [NAS.RH15.91.60]

HOLLAND, DAVID, 1694. [NAS.RH15.91.60]

HOLMES, JOHN, master of the John of Belfast at the port of Ayr on 3 September 1667. [NAS.E71.3.2]

HOME, WILLIAM, in Drumbeg, Ireland, 1707
  [NAS.RS.Berwick#7/262]; portioner of Hornden, 1718.
  [NAS.RS.Berwick#9/257]

HORNER, BESSIE, from Kirkmahoe, Dumfries-shire, moved to
  Ireland before 1659. [Mouswald parish KSR]

HOUETT, WILLIAM, 1694. [NAS.RH15.91.60]

HOULT, LILLIE, a servant, 1694. [NAS.RH15.91.60]

HOUSTON, ROBERT, a merchant in Silver Street, Londonderry,
  1659. [C]

HOUSTON, WILLIAM, a gentleman in Galgorme, Barony of
  Toome, County Antrim, 1659. [C]

HOUSTOUN, LUDOVICK, of Ardmalin, Barony of Inishaven,
  County Donegal, 1707. [NAS.CC8.8.84/162]

HOW, JOHN, at White Hart, Wellbrook, County Tyrone, 1689.
  [NAS.GD26.8.16]

HOWIE, the widow, in the Barony of Glenarm, 1650s.
  [NAS.GD154.512]

HUEISON, JAMES, in Dublin, 1672. [NAS.RH16.91.62]

HUGH, ..., in the Barony of Glenarm, 1650s. [NAS.GD154.512]

HUME, ALEXANDER, was granted the lands of Drumcoas, in the
  Barony of Maghereboye, County Fermanagh, on 4 September
  1610. [TCD]

HUME, GEORGE, an undertaker in County Fermanagh, with 1000
  acres, 28 men, 21 swords, 7 pikes, 1 muskets, etc. [1641
  Muster Roll of Ulster]

HUME, Sir JOHN, was granted lands in the Barony of
  Maghereboye, County Fermanagh, 23 August 1610. [TCD]

HUME, Sir JOHN, an undertaker in County Fermanagh, with 3500 acres, 88 men, 52 swords, 37 pikes, etc. [1641 Muster Roll of Ulster]

HUME, THOMAS, of Bairrie, County Cavan, 10 June 1693. [NAS.GD1/420.10]

HUNTER, HENRY, from County Armagh, Captain of a company of soldiers, to return from Scotland to Ireland in 1689. [RPCS.XIII.425]

HUNTER, JOHN, master of the Marian of Glenarm at the port of Ayr on 29 October 1673. [NAS.E71.3.3]

HUNTER, JOHN, a minister who fled from Ireland in 1689, settled in Kirkmichael, Ayrshire, by 1691. [RPCS.XVI.336]

HUNTER, JOHN, a minister at Bonvery, Ireland, was, by the right of his father the late Robert Hunter former Provost of Ayr, admitted as a burgess and guilds-brother of Ayr on 8 November 1692. [ABR]

HUNTER, ..., in the Barony of Antrim, 1659. [C]

HUTCHEON, ARCHIBALD, a gentleman in Scronokrum, parish of Bellemone, County Antrim, 1659. [C]

HUTCHEON, THOMAS, in Irvine, was alleged to have supplied weapons to the rebels in Ireland, 1601. [RPCS.V.324]

HUTCHISON, ALEXANDER, a Presbyterian minister in northern Ireland, 1679. [RPCS.VI.657]

HUTCHISON, JAMES, merchant on the James of Glenarm from Ayr to Belfast on 7 February 1691. [NAS.E72.3.26]

HUTCHISON, JOHN, 1674, 1694. [NAS.RH15.91.60]

HUY, JOHN, late sergeant of Lord Barganie's Company in Ireland, fought at Killileoch against the forces of King James, by 1689. [RPCS.XIV.316]

IRVING, CHRISTOPHER, of Castle Irving, Ireland, MD, only child of Christopher Irving MD in Edinburgh, and his wife Margaret, daughter of late James Wishart of Pitarrow, versus Elizabeth Ker in Edinburgh, John son of the late Christopher Irving, Sydney Carleton, relict of the late Thomas Irvine in Edinburgh, etc. Christopher Irving and Margaret Wishart married in Ireland in 1639. They had three children Christopher, James, and Gerard, baptised at South Leith on 3 February 1650. Thomas Irving and John Irving were sons of late Dr Christopher Irving and Jean Ker, born in adultery. Margaret Wishart died in Ireland during February 1689. [NAS.CC8.Consistorial Processes, 6 August 1695]

IRVING, JAMES, an undertaker in County Longford, 1621. [RPCS.XII.420]

IRVING, JOHN, in Kilbryde, was alleged to have supplied weapons to the rebels in Ireland, 1601. [RPCS.V.324]

IRVING, LUDOVICK, of Wisbie, a thief from the Borders, was captured in Ireland during 1679. [RPCS.VI.158]

IRVING, RICHARD, of Woodhouse, was banished from Scotland to Ireland by the Privy Council on 10 June 1620. [RPCS.XII.288]

IRVING, ..., in County Fermanagh, 1659. [C]

JACKSON, CORNELIUS, a surgeon, son of late James Jackson a surgeon in Londonderry, 1690. [RPCS.XV.381]

JACKSON, HERCULES, leased the townland of Dingonie, parish of Dunboe, County Londonderry, on 30 June 1655. [NAS.RH15.91.59]

JAMIESON, ALEXANDER, master of the Bonadventure of Donaghadie, at the port of Ayr on 14 February 1667. [NAS.E71.3.1]

JAMIESON, ROBERT, an alleged pirate from Ayr, was accused of looting the cargo on a ship of Thomas Copran, a merchant in Dublin, off northern Ireland in 1586. [RPCS.IV.72]

JAMIESON, WILLIAM, a gentleman in Letterkenny town, parish of Conwall, Barony of Killmccrenan, County Donegal, 1659. [C]

JOHNSTON, ADAM, in Belfast, 1689. [NAS.GD26.13.385]

JOHNSTON, ALEXANDER, a gentleman in Ballywilly, parish of Rathry, County Antrim, 1659. [C]

JOHNSTON, JOHN, leased the townland of Gorticaron, parish of Dunboe, County Londonderry, on 12 June 1655. [NAS.RH15.91.59]

JOHNSTON, ..., in County Fermanagh, 1659. [C]

JOHNSTONE, ANDREW, a thief from the Scottish Borders who was apprehended in Ireland and returned to Scotland, where he was imprisoned in Dumfries Tolbooth in 1632. [RPCS.IV.496]

JOHNSTONE, ARCHIBALD, of Howgill, was banished from Scotland by the Privy Council on 10 June 1620. [RPCS.XII.288]

JOHNSTONE, JANE, 1694. [NAS.RH15.91.60]

JOHNSTONE, JOHN, from Drysdale, Dumfries-shire, a merchant in Carrickfergus, who died by November 1679, father of William. [NAS.SH.27.11.1679]

JOHNSTONE, PATRICK, a merchant in Dublin, was admitted as a burgess and guilds-brother of Ayr on 22 June 1711. [ABR]

JOHNSTONE, RICHARD, a passenger on the Speedwell of Glenarm at the port of Ayr on 24 June 1673. [NAS.E71.3.3]

JOHNSTONE, ROBERT, of Leverhay, was banished from Scotland by the Privy Council on 10 June 1620. [RPCS.XII.288]

JOHNSTONE, ROBERT, in Artikillie (?), 16... [NAS.RH15.91.49]

JOHNSTONE, THOMAS, leased the townland of Gorticaron, parish of Dunboe, County Londonderry, on 12 June 1655. [NAS.RH15.91.59]

JOHNSTONE, WILLIAM, in Ireland, 1659. [NAS.RD{C&S}, 605/233]

JOHNSTONE, WILLIAM, 1694. [NAS.RH15.91.60]

KELSO, GARVEN, of Hollywood, County Down, 1617. [NAS.RH15.91.59/2]

KELSO, JAMES, imprisoned in Glasgow on arrival from Ireland, 1685. [RPCS.XI.66]

KELSO, Mr SAMUEL, sometime minister at Whithorn and Kirkmaben in Galloway, then at Dinochcloney, County Down, testament confirmed on 28 June 1698 with the Commissariat of Edinburgh. [NAS]

KELSO, THOMAS, in Bellchachanner, County Down, 1617. [NAS.RD1.301]

KENDALL, JAMES, a prisoner brought from Ireland to Scotland in 1690. [RPCS.XV.278]

KENNEDY, AGNES, daughter of Sir Alexander Kennedy of Culzean, and spouse of Captain James Hamilton in Nilsbruike, County Antrim, 1677. [NAS.GD25/SEC8/666]

KENNEDY, ANTHONY, in Moncloynt, parish of Ray, Barony of Rapho, County Donegal, 1659. [C]

KENNEDY, DAVID, in Newton, Ireland, 10 January 1645. [NAS.CH1/5/4/27]

KENNEDY, Captain DAVID, sent to Ireland in 1691 to gather intelligence. [RPCS.XVI.73]

KENNEDY, HORATIUS, Sheriff of Londonderry in 1689, [RPCS.XIII.392]; Alderman of Londonderry, was admitted as a burgess and guilds-brother of Ayr on 9 April 1694. [ABR]

KENNEDY, M., of Newton, 1694. [NAS.RH15.91.60]

KENNEDY, P. P., in Killyreagh, County Down, 1675.
[NAS.RH15.91.59]

KENNEDY, QUINTIN, in Bellihomage, Ireland, 1671.
[NAS.GD180.255]

KENNEDY, ROBERT, a gentleman in Torninrobert, parish of
Armoy, County Antrim, 1659. [C]

KENNEDY, THOMAS, a minister in Newtonards, County Down,
1675, [NAS.RH15.91.59]; a Presbyterian minister in northern
Ireland, 1679. [RPCS.VI.657]

KENNEDY, ..., in the Barony of Antrim, 1659. [C]

KENNEDY, ..., in the Barony of Belfast, County Antrim, 1659.
[C]

KENNEDY, ..., in the Barony of Toome, County Antrim, 1659.
[C]

KENNEDY, ... in the Barony of Rapho, County Donegal, 1659.
[C]

KER, DANIEL, a leasee in the parish of Rapho, County Donegal,
1654. [CS]

KER, JAMES, a Protestant and leasee in the parish of Rapho,
County Donegal, 1654. [CS]

KERR, GILBERT, a plotter and rebel in Ireland, 1663.
[RPCS.I.371]

KERR, JOHN, in the Barony of Glenarm, 1650s, tenant in the
parish of Kilwaghter, 1660s?. [NAS.GD154.512/525]

KERR, MICHAEL, a gentleman in Carrickfergus, County Antrim,
1659. [C]

KERR, WILLIAM, an undertaker in County Longford, 1621. [RPCS.XII.420]

KIDD, JAMES, in Kilwaghter, 1690, 1691. [NAS.GD154.527/1, 528]

KILPATRICK, ROBERT, in Artikillie (?), 16... [NAS.RH15.91.49]

KILPATRICK, ..., in the Barony of Toome, County Antrim, 1659. [C]

KINCADE, CLAUDE, a Protestant and freeholder of Shragolan, parish of Camos, Barony of Strabane, County Tyrone, 1654. [CS]

KINCAID, JOHN, master of the <u>Hopewell of Carrickfergus</u>, was admitted as a burgess and guilds-brother of Ayr on 22 June 1722. [ABR]

KING, JOHN, in the Barony of Glenarm, 1650s. [NAS.GD154.512]

KNOX, ALEXANDER, a gentleman in Killigadan, parish of Donoghmore, Barony of Rapho, County Donegal, 1659. [C]

KNOX, ANDREW, a Protestant and proprietor in the parish of Killgarvan, Barony of Killmaccrenan, County Donegal, 1654. [CS]

KNOX, GEORGE, a Protestant and leasee in the parish of Rapho, and in the parish of Drumhome, County Donegal, 1654. [CS]; in Ballinagunnenagh, parish of Drumhome, 1659. [C]

KNOX, HUGH, in Kilwaghter, 1690. [NAS.GD154.527/1]

KNOX, JAMES, a Protestant gentleman in the parish of Clandevadock, County Donegal, 1654. [CS]

KNOX, JAMES, a gentleman in Killmore, parish of Gartan, Barony of Killmccrenan, County Donegal, 1659. [C]

KNOX, JOHN, in the Barony of Glenarm, 1650s.
[NAS.GD154.512/515]

KNOX, JOHN, a leasee in the parish of Rapho, County Donegal,
dead by 1654. [CS]

KNOX, JOHN, a Protestant in the parish of Gartan, Barony of
Killmaccrenan, County Donegal, 1654. [CS]

KNOX, ROBERT, tenant of 20 acres in Drumahoe, parish of
Kilwaghter, 1690, 1692, 1695.
[NAS.GD154.525/527/530/532]

KNOX, THOMAS, in Tagonan, parish of Maglas, Barony of Forth,
County Wexford, 1659. [C]

KNOX, THOMAS, in Belfast, was admitted as a burgess and
guilds-brother of Ayr on 23 February 1695. [ABR]

KNOX, WILLIAM, an undertaker in County Longford, 1621.
[RPCS.XII.420]

KNOX, WILLIAM, sheriff of County Donegal, 1672.
[NAS.GD10.495]

KNOX, WILLIAM, 1702. [NAS.GD154.532]

KNOX, Major, a gentleman in Ray, parish of Auchnish, Barony of
Killmccrenan, County Donegal, 1659. [C]

KYLE, ARCHIBALD, a Protestant and leasee in the parish of
Rapho, County Donegal, 1654. [CS]

KYLE, JAMES, in Glasgow, was alleged to have supplied
weapons to the rebels in Ireland, 1601. [RPCS.V.324]

LAMOND, JOHN, master of the Blessing of Belfast at the port of
Ayr in December 1666, also in June 1667; master of the
Salmon of Belfast at the port of Ayr on 30 September 1667.
[NAS.E71.3.1/2]

LANARK, JOHN, a shoemaker, 1674. [NAS.RH15.91.60]

LANARK, the widow, 1675. [NAS.RH15.91.60]

LANG, WILLIAM, leased the townland of Glasentarny, parish of Dunboe, County Londonderry, on 13 July 1655. [NAS.RH15.91.59]

LAUDER, WILLIAM, was granted 1000 acres in Kilruddan in the precinct of Feus, County Armagh, on 26 April 1610. [TCD]

LAWSON, WILLIAM, a gentleman in Kilkighan, parish of Kilamarde, Barony of Roylagh and Banagh, County Donegal, 1659. [C]

LAWTIN, ROBERT, in the Barony of Glenarm, 1650s. [NAS.GD154.512]

LEARMOND, ADAM, in the parish of Killamen, Barony of Dungannon, County Tyrone, dead by 1654. [CS]

LECKY, ALEXANDER, a merchant and alderman of Londonderry in 1689. [RPCS,XIII.392]

LECKY, JAMES, a gentleman in the parish of Leck, Barony of Rapho, County Donegal, 1659. [C]

LECKY, THOMAS, in the parish of Ray, County Donegal, 1654. [CS]

LECKY, THOMAS, born 1705, died 1 May 1780. [Ballymoney g/s, County Antrim]

LECKY, WALTER, an undertaker in County Longford, 1621. [RPCS.XII.420]

LEE, JAMES, master of the Mary of Cork, from Scotland to Cork in 1716; from Cromarty to Cork in 1716. [NAS.E502/E508]

LEEPER, JOHN, 1694. [NAS.RH15.91.60]

LEGGAT, WILLIAM, a Presbyterian minister in northern Ireland, 1679. [RPCS.VI.657]

LEICH, THOMAS, tenant of 10 acres in Drumadonachan, parish of Kilwaghter, 1690, 1692, 1695. [NAS.GD154.525/530/532]

LEITH, DUNCAN, a fisher in Glasgow, was alleged to have supplied weapons to the rebels in Ireland, 1601. [RPCS.V.324]

LEITH, FLORE, tenant in Drumnadonachie, May 1645. [NAS.GD154.509]; tenant of 30 acres in the Barony of Glenarm, 1650s. [NAS.GD154.512/515]

LEITH, JOHN, a fisher in Glasgow, was alleged to have supplied weapons to the rebels in Ireland, 1601. [RPCS.V.324]

LEITHES, WILLIAM, in Newton, Ireland, 10 January 1645. [NAS.CH1/5/4/27]

LENNOX, Duke of, an undertaker in County Donegal, with 4000 acres, 166 men, 100 swords, 14 pikes, etc. [1641 Muster Roll of Ulster]

LENNOX, JAMES, of Carshewy, Parish of Taboyne, County Donegal, 1654. [CS]

LENNOX, JAMES, a merchant in Silver Street, Londonderry, 1659. [C]

LENNOX, JOHN, in Londonderry, was admitted as a burgess and guilds-brother of Ayr on 3 September 1706. [ABR]

LENNOX, ROBERT, a merchant in Belfast, 1676; a yeoman in Belfast, 1678. [NAS.GD10.819/823]

LENNOX, ROBERT, possibly from Earlston, settled in Drumboin, Ireland, by 1685, by 1691 in Londonderry. [NAS.GD10.532/533]

LENNOX, WILLIAM, of Carshewy, Parish of Taboyne, County Donegal, 1654. [CS]

LENNOX, WILLIAM, a gentleman in the parish of Ray, Barony of Rapho, County Donegal, 1659. [C]

LESLIE, JAMES, in Artikillie (?), 16... [NAS.RH15.91.49]

LESLIE, JOHN, Bishop of Raphoe, 1623-1647.
[NAS.GD188/21/3]

LESLY, JOHN, a leasee in the parish of Rapho, County Donegal,
dead before 1654. [CS]

LESLY, Dr JOHN, a Protestant and leasee in the parish of Rapho,
County Donegal, 1654. [CS]

LESLY, WILLIAM, a gentleman in Dunmurray and the Fall,
Barony of Belfast, County Antrim, 1659. [C]

LILBOURNE, JOHN, in the Barony of Glenarm, 1650s, tenant of
33 acres in the parish of Kilwaghter, 1660s.
[NAS.GD154.512]

LILBOURNE, JOHN, the younger, in the Barony of Glenarm,
1650s. [NAS.GD154.512]

LILBURNE, JOHN, tenant of 33 acres in the parish of Kilwaghter,
1690. [NAS.GD154.525]

LINDSAY, BERNARD, via Ayr to Ireland in 1609. [Ayr Burgh
Accounts]

LINDSAY, BERNARD, was granted 1000 acres of Creige in the
precinct of Mountjoy, County Tyrone, on 19 April 1610, and
part of Tullaghoge in the precinct of Mountjoy, County
Tyrone, 6 September 1610. [TCD]

LINDSAY, BERNARD, a Protestant, in the parish of derrygloran,
Barony of Dungannon, County Tyrone, 1654. [CS]

LINDSAY, JAMES, a gentleman in Maymore, parish of
Taghboine, Barony of Rapho, County Donegal, 1659. [C]

LINDSAY, JOHN, 1694. [NAS.RH15.91.60]

LINDSAY, MATHEW, a gentleman in Maymore, parish of
Taghboine, Barony of Rapho, County Donegal, 1659. [C]

LINDSAY, ROBERT, of Leith, granted part of Tullaghoge in the precinct of Mountjoy, County Tyrone, 6 September 1610. [TCD]

LINDSAY, ROBERT, of Korton, was granted 1000 acres of Gartavillye in the precinct of Mountjoy, County Tyrone, on 9 April 1610. [TCD]

LINDSAY, ROBERT, a minister residing in the Glebe lands of the parish of Killbeggs, County Donegal, 1654. [CS]

LINDSAY, ROBERT, a Protestant and proprietor in the parishes of Donaghenry, and of Derrygloran, Barony of Dungannon, County Tyrone, 1654. [CS]

LINDSAY, ROBERT, in Artikillie (?), 16... [NAS.RH15.91.49]

LINDSAY, WILLIAM, minister at Dreghorn, fled to Ireland with his wife in 1648. [RPCS.I.291]

LINDSAY, WILLIAM, 1694. [NAS.RH15.91.60]

LINDSAY, Mrs, widow of Robert Lindsay, in Tullahoge, 1622. [BL.Add.MS#4756/52/12]

LINTON, ROBERT, in Artikillie (?), 16... [NAS.RH15.91.49]

LITTLE, JOHN, a resident of Ireland and servant of the Earl of Nithsdale, 1631. [RPCS.IV.660]

LIVINGSTON, JOHN, an officer of the Danish Force in Ireland, 1689-1691. [DFI#146]

LOCHNOREIS, Lord, was granted 1000 acres of Tullelagan in the precinct of Mountjoy, County Tyrone, on 9 April 1610. [TCD]

LOGAN, WALTER, merchant of the Swallow of Coleraine at the port of Ayr on 1 February 1673. [NAS.E71.3.3]

LOGAN, ..., in the Barony of Antrim, 1659. [C]

LOGAN, ..., in the Barony of Belfast, County Antrim, 1659. [C]

LOGAN, ..., in the Barony of Toome, County Antrim, 1659. [C]

LOGAN, ..., in Carrickfergus, 1659. [C]

LORBART, JOHN, 1694. [NAS.RH15.91.60]

LOUDEN, JAMES, 1694. [NAS.RH15.91.60]

LOUDEN, JOHN, 1694. [NAS.RH15.91.60]

LOURIE, JANE, 1694. [NAS.RH15.91.60]

LOURIE, THOMAS, 1694. [NAS.RH15.91.60]

LOW, JAMES, in the Barony of Glenarm, 1650s. [NAS.GD154.512]

LOWRIE, ALEXANDER, in Irvine, was alleged to have supplied weapons to the rebels in Ireland, 1601. [RPCS.V.324]

LOWRIE, ..., in Kilbryde, was alleged to have supplied weapons to the rebels in Ireland, 1601. [RPCS.V.324]

LUMSDEN, ANNA, daughter of Alexander Lumsden of Aflect, then in Killicarne, Ireland, 8 July 1697. [NAS.GD108.54]

LYELL, MARION, spouse of James Kennedy a messenger formerly in Maybole then in Bellicastle, Ireland, 1622. [NAS.RS.Ayr#2/395]

LYN, WILLIAM, in the parish of Rapho, County Donegal, only son and heir of the deceased Margaret Muir, 23 November 1665, and 31 July 1666. [NAS.GD1/693/13, 15]

LYNE, DAVID, a Protestant and proprietor in the parish of Clandevadock, Barony of Killmaccrenan, County Donegal, 1654. [CS]

LYNE, WILLIAM, a Protestant and proprietor in the parish of Clandevadock, Barony of Killmaccrenan, County Donegal, 1654. [CS]

LYNN, WILLIAM, a Protestant, heir to his uncle William Lyon in the lands of Cloghogall, parish of Donoghkiddy, County Tyrone, 1654.[CS]

LYSLEY, JOHN, the elder, a Protestant and a proprietor in the parish of Donoghkiddy, Barony of Strabane, 1654. [CS]

MCALEXANDER, THOMAS, the Provost of Strabane, County Tyrone, 1631. [NAS.E661.142]

MCALESTER, ..., in the Barony of Antrim, 1659. [C]

MCBONE, IVOR, in the Barony of Glenarm, 1650s. [NAS.GD154.512]

MCBRAIR, DAVID, of Newark, Kirkcudbrightshire, to Ireland by 1665. [RPCS.II.58]

MCBRIDE, DAVID, a merchant in Belfast, was admitted as a burgess and guilds-brother of Ayr on 6 September 1715. [ABR]

MCBRIDE, JOHN, in Belfast, 7 July 1704. [NAS.CH1/5/6/186]

MCBROOM, JOHN, a Presbyterian minister in northern Ireland, 1679. [RPCS.VI.657]

MCCAIGHIE, PATRICK, rent collector in Kilwaghter, 1690-1693. [NAS.GD154.527/1]

MCCAIGHIE, WILLIAM, tenant of 6 acres in the parish of Kilwaghter, 1660s. [NAS.GD154.525.2/2]

MCCALLEY, BRIAN, in the Barony of Glenarm, 1650s. [NAS.GD154.512]

MCCAMOCH, JAMES, in Artikillie, 1695 [NAS.RH15.91.49]

MCCAR.(?), THOMAS, tenant of 50 acres in the Barony of Glenarm, 1650s. [NAS.GD154.512/515]

MCCARTNEY, GEORGE, in Belfast, 1674, 1679. [NAS.RH15.91.60]

MCCARTNEY, GEORGE, a merchant in Belfast, 1691, [RPCS.XVI.309]; was admitted as a burgess and guilds-brother of Ayr on 4 July 1697. [ABR]

MCCARTNEY, ..., in the Barony of Belfast, County Antrim, 1659. [C]

MCCAUSLAND, ROBERT, a Protestant refugee from Ireland, in Edinburgh 1689. [RPCS.XIII.410]

MCCAW, JOHN, in the Barony of Glenarm, 1650s. [NAS.GD154.512]

MCCHACHIE, PATRICK, tenant of 11 acres in Lelish, parish of Kilwaghter, 1690; receipt dated 18 November 1693. [NAS.GD154.525/527]

MCCHACHIE, WILLIAM, tenant in Leales, May 1645. [NAS.GD154.509]

MCCHALME, GEORGE, tenant of 20 acres in the parish of Kilwaghter, 1660s. [NAS.GD154.525.2/2]

MCCHE, WILLIAM, tenant of 6 acres in Barony of Glenarm, 1653. [NAS.GD154/515]

MCCLARTIE, NEILL, moved from Argyll to Ireland before 1654. [RSA#2/71]

MCCLAY, RONALD, a gentleman in Diskerteavne, parish of Finboy, County Antrim, 1659. [C]

MCCLELLAN, ANN, 1694. [NAS.RH15.91.60]

MCCLELLAN, EDWARD, in Artikillie , 16... [NAS.RH15.91.49]

MCCLELLAN, HARRY, in Artikillie, 16... [NAS.RH15.91.49]

MCCLELLAN, JOHN, of Borge, freeholder of Mean, Ercolah, 1619. [NAS.RH15.91.33]

MCCLELLAN, JOHN, of the Orchard, freeholder of Ballemonnivonne, 1619. [NAS.RH15.91.33]

MCCLELLAN, JOHN, of Barlocko, a resident of Ireland by 1636. [NAS.RD.498, 17.11.1636]

MACCLELLAN, ROBERT, of Bombie, in Ballelandbegg and in Ballecullieseger, west side of the River Laggan, County Down, 1611. [NAS.212, 1.7.1613]

MCCLELLAN, THOMAS, a gentleman in Carrickfergus, County Antrim, 1659. [C]

MCCLELLAN, WILLIAM, of Overlaw, freeholder of Dromlesse, 1619. [NAS.RH15.91.33]

MCCLELLAN, WILLIAM, of Molock, freeholder of Ballemonnivonne, 1619. [NAS.RH15.91.33]

MCCLELLAN, WILLIAM, 1673. [NAS.RH15.91.60]

MCCLELLAND, ADAM, a gentleman in Craford, parish of Killmccrenan, County Donegal, 1659. [C]

MCCLELLAND, JOHN, leased the townland of Donallees, parish of Dunboe, County Londonderry, on 24 July 1655. [NAS.RH15.91.59]

MCCLELLAND, JOHN, in Artikillie (?), 16... [NAS.RH15.91.49]

MCCLELLAND, ROBERT, leased the townland of Ballanteirmore, parish of Macaskie, County Londonderry, on 29 August 1655. [NAS.RH15.91.59]

MCCLELLAND, WILLIAM, of Carrickobilt, County Londonderry, 1638. [NAS.RH15.91.59]

MCCLELLAND, WILLIAM, leased the townland of Exorna, parish of Dunboe, County Londonderry, on 8 September 1655. [NAS.RH15.91.59]

MCCLELLAND, WILLIAM, in Artikillie, 1695
[NAS.RH15.91.49]

MCCLELAND, ..., in the Barony of Belfast, County Antrim,
1659. [C]

MCCLOE, DONALD, in the Barony of Glenarm, 1650s.
[NAS.GD154.512]

MCCLURGE, PATRICK, 1694. [NAS.RH15.91.60]

MCCOLLO, JAMES, a gentleman on Island Magee, Barony of
Belfast, County Antrim, 1659. [C]

MCCOLLUM, ROBERT, in the Barony of Glenarm, 1650s.
[NAS.GD154.512]

MCCONNACHY, DANIEL, master of the Marie of Coleraine,
from Port Glasgow to Coleraine on 20 April 1681.
[NAS.E72.19.2]

MCCONNELL, ANGUS, of Donnyveg, from Kintyre, Argyll, to
Ireland in 1595. [CSPS.XII.94][RPCS.V.393]

MCCONNELL, JOHN, 1694. [NAS.RH15.91.60]

MCCORMICK, ..., in the Barony of Antrim, 1659. [C]

MCCRAE, JOHN, a seaman of Belfast, to be released from
Edinburgh or Canongate Tolbooth in July 1689.
[RPCS.XIII.554]

MCCREERIE, ROBERT, 1694. [NAS.RH15.91.60]

MCCREERY, ..., in the Barony of Belfast, County Antrim,
1659. [C]

MCCUBBIN, JOHN, of Belhannie, and also of County Antrim,
testament confirmed 29 December 1696 with the
Commissariat of Glasgow. [NAS]

MCCULLAN, JAMES, 1668, 1694. [NAS.RH15.91.60]

MCCULLOCH, JAMES, was granted part of Mulloneaghe in the precinct of Boylaghe, County Donegal, on 9 September 1610. [TCD]

MCCULLOCH, JOHN, 1702. [NAS.GD154.533/10]

MCCULLOCH, WILLIAM, a gentleman in the Lyne of Mounteredy, Barony of Toome, County Antrim, 1659. [C]

MCCULLOCH, WILLIAM, of Clanbuie, Ireland, was admitted as a burgess and guilds-brother of Ayr on 3 November 1705. [ABR]

MCCULLOGH, DAVID, a Protestant, leasee in the parish of Tulloghobegly, Barony of Killmaccrenan, County Donegal, dead by 1654. [CS]

MCCULLOUGH, ..., in the Barony of Antrim, 1659. [C]

MCCUN, JAMES, master of the Marie of Hollywood arrived in Port Glasgow on 11 March 1681 from Belfast. [NAS.E72.19.1]

MCDARE, JOHN, tenant of 6 acres in the parish of Kilwaghter, 1660s? [NAS.GD154.525.2/2]

MCDOELL, JOHN, a debtor in 1702. [NAS.GD154.532]

MCDONALD, Sir DONALD, of Sleat, was licenced to go to Ireland for one year on 31 July 1623. [RPCS.XIII.318]

MCDOUGALL, ..., in the Barony of Toome, County Antrim, 1659. [C]

MCDOWELL, JOHN, a seaman of Belfast, to be released from Edinburgh or Canongate Tolbooth in July 1689. [RPCS.XIII.554]

MCDOWELL, ..., in the Barony of Castlereagh, County Down, 1659. [C]

MCEUEN, ARCHIBALD, married Marie NcInleastere, in Ireland and returned to Argyll, Scotland, before 1657. [RSA#2/162]

MCFARLAN, JOHN, a Protestant refugee from Ireland, in Edinburgh 1689. [RPCS.XIII.410]

MCGEE, JOHN, 1694. [NAS.RH15.91.60]

MCGIE, ROBERT, in the Barony of Glenarm, 1650s, tenant in the parish of Kilwaghter, 1660s. [NAS.GD154.512/525]

MCGILL, C., in the Barony of Glenarm, 1650s. [NAS.GD154.512]

MCGILL, DONALD, in the Barony of Glenarm, 1650s. [NAS.GD154.512]

MCGILL, GILDUFF, in the Barony of Glenarm, 1650s. [NAS.GD154.512]

MCGILL, JOHN, in the Barony of Glenarm, 1650s. [NAS.GD154.512]

MCGILL, JOHN, master of the Joan of Belfast, arrived in Port Glasgow on 22 December 1681 from Belfast. [NAS.E72.19.5]

MCGILL, JOHN, in Artikillie (?), 16... [NAS.RH15.91.49]

MCGILL, NEAL, a witness in Glenarm, 15 August 1659. [NAS.GD154.522]

MCGILL, PATRICK, in the Barony of Glenarm, 1650s. [NAS.GD154.512]

MCHERON, JOHN, a seaman of Belfast, to be released from Edinburgh or Canongate Tolbooth in July 1689. [RPCS.XIII.554]

MCILMARTIN, DUNCAN, in Kilbryde, was alleged to have supplied weapons to the rebels in Ireland, 1601. [RPCS.V.324]

MCILROY, ..., in the Barony of Antrim, 1659. [C]

MCILWEE, GILBERT, a Protestant and proprietor in the parish of Conwall, County Donegal, 1654. [CS]; in Letterkenny town, parish of Conwall, 1659. [C]

MACKAY, ALEXANDER, in Kilwaghter parish, 1692. [NAS.GD154.530]

MCKAY, ..., in the Barony of Toome, County Antrim, 1659. [C]

MCKAY, ..., in the Barony of Enishowen, County Donegal, 1659. [C]

MCKECHY, PATRICK, tenant of 13 acres in Lelis, 1695. [NAS.GD154.532]

MCKEE, ALEXANDER, 1694. [NAS.RH15.91.60]

MCKEE, Sir PATRICK, was granted part of Cargy in the precinct of Boylaghe, County Donegal, on 9 September 1610. [TCD]

MCKENIE, JOHN, a seaman of Belfast, to be released from Edinburgh or Canongate Tolbooth in July 1689. [RPCS.XIII.554]

MCKENZIE, ALEXANDER, tenant of 62 acres in Drumnadonachan, parish of Kilwaghter, 1690, 1692. [NAS.GD154.525/527/530]

MCKENZIE, JOHN, a minister of the parish of Urra who fled to England around 1639 and later moved to Ireland. [RPCS.I.163]

MCKEOWN, THOMAS, 1702. [NAS.GD154.532]

MCKEY, DANIEL, a Protestant and a proprietor in the parish of Donoghkiddy, Barony of Strabane, County Tyrome, 1654. [CS]

MCKEY, HUGH, a Protestant and a proprietor in the parish of Donoghkiddy, Barony of Strabane, County Tyrome, 1654. [CS]

MCKIE, JAMES, in Carshowy, parish of Taboyne, County Donegal, 1654. [CS]

MCKIE, JOHN, 1694. [NAS.RH15.91.60]

MCKIE, THOMAS, a merchant burgess of Belfast, was serviced as heir to his father Patrick McKie of Cairn, Wigtonshire, on 25 September 1688. [NAS.SH.5.9.1688]

MCKILLIWICK. MATHEW, 1673. [NAS.RH15.91.60]

MCKINLAY, ..., in the Barony of Toome, County Antrim, 1659. [C]

MCKINNY, DAVID, in Glasgow, was alleged to have supplied weapons to the rebels in Ireland, 1601. [RPCS.V.324]

MCKINNY, NORMAN, in Glasgow, was alleged to have supplied weapons to the rebels in Ireland, 1601. [RPCS.V.324]

MCKNAIGHT, WILLIAM, 1673. [NAS.RH15.91.60]

MCKYE, ..., in the Barony of Antrim, 1659. [C]

MCLELAND, JOHN, senior, in Ardekelly, County Londonderry, 1664. [NAS.RH15.91.16]

MCLELAND, JOHN, junior, in Ardekelly, County Londonderry, 1664. [NAS.RH15.91.16]

MCLELAND, Sir ROBERT, of Bombie, was ordered to raise 50 horsemen and 100 foot soldiers and take them to Ireland, 22 November 1625. [RPCS.I.196]

MCLELAND, Sir ROBERT, in Londonderry, with 6000 acres, 192 men, 118 swords, 54 pikes, 1 muskets, etc. [1641 Muster Roll of Ulster]

MCLELAND, THOMAS, a Protestant and proprietor in the parish of Dunboe, Barony of Coleraine, County Londonderry, 1654. [CS]

MCLUNN, WILLIAM, a servant of William Hamilton of Killeach in Ireland, was admitted as a burgess and guilds-brother of Ayr on 25 September 1699. [ABR]

MCMARENS, FERGUS, a tenant of 2 acres in the parish of Kilwaghter, 1660s. [NAS.GD154.525.2/2]

MCMARTIN, SHAWN, tenant of 6 acres in the parish of Kilwaghter, 1660s. [NAS.GD154.525.2/2]

MCMATH, FREDERICK, a merchant in Londonderry, 1664. [RPCS.I.487]

MCMATH, JOHN, a merchant in Belfast, was admitted as a burgess and guilds-brother of Ayr on 16 August 1697. [ABR]

MCMIKAN, WILLIAM, tenant of 62 acres in Drumnadonachan, parish of Kilwaghter, 1690, 1692, 1695. [NAS.GD154.525/530/532]

MACMILLAN, JOHN, in Casholloch, Ireland, 1663. [RPCS.1.360/361/379]

MCMIM, JAMES, 1694. [NAS.RH15.91.60]

MCMOLLANE, JANE, from Rockall, Mouswald parish, moved to Ireland before 1659. [Mouswald KSR]

MCMULLAN, ANDREW, in Artikillie (?), 16... [NAS.RH15.91.49]

MCMULLAN, ANTHONY, in Artikillie, 1695 [NAS.RH15.91.49]

MCNAIGHT, MARGARET, 1694. [NAS.RH15.91.60]

MCNARE, PATRICK, a Protestant and leasee in the parish of Rapho, County Donegal, dead by 1654. [CS]

MCNEALL, Lieutenant DANIEL, a gentleman in Ballycastle, parish of Ramoan, County Antrim, 1659. [C]

MCNEILL, JEAN, daughter of Archibald McNeill of Clogar, Rector of Ballentoy, Ireland, 1704. [NAS.RS.Argyll#3/418]

MCNEILL, LAUCHLAN, son of Neill McNeill of Killquezen, Tarum, Ireland, 1701. [NAS.RS.Argyll, 3/222]

MCNEILL, MALCOLM, of Ballimukscanland, Ireland, 1702. [NAS.RS.Argyll#3/283]

MCNICOLL, LACHLAN, and Moira NcNicoll, went from Argyll to Ireland to marry in 1653. [RSA#2/26]

MCPATRECK, the widow, a sub-tenant of Robert Montgomery in County Armagh in 1622. [NLI.ms8014/ix]

MCPHETRISH, ARCHIBALD, a gentleman in Carnglass, parish of Ballywillin, County Antrim, 1659. [C]

MACRAE, THOMAS, in the Barony of Glenarm, 1650s. [NAS.GD154.512]

MCRONNELL, JAMES, a maltster, 1694. [NAS.RH15.91.60]

MCTIER, JOHN, a seaman of Belfast, to be released from Edinburgh or Canongate Tolbooth in July 1689. [RPCS.XIII.554]

MCWILLIAM, JOHN, master of the Janet of Belfast, from Cromarty, Scotland, to Stockholm, Sweden, in 1716. [NAS.E502/E508]

MACWILLIAMSON, PHILLIP, master of the James of Donaghadie at the port of Kirkcudbright on 8 September 1673. [NAS.E71.6.2]

MADER, ROBERT, of Dungannan, a gentleman, around 1675. [NAS.RH9.17.103]

MAGRAMEL, (?), RORY, in the Barony of Glenarm, 1650s. [NAS.GD154.512]

MAKINSHIRE, JAMES, leased the townland of Ballymoney, parish of Dunboe, County Londonderry, on 4 September 1655. [NAS.RH15.91.59]

MARSHALL, Captain JAMES. Process of Divorce, Anna, second daughter of Sir Robert Montgomery of Skelmorlie, against Captain James Marshall, late a merchant in Newportoun, County Fermanagh, married in February 1692 in Edinburgh. [NAS.CC8.Consistorial Processes, 2 February 1693]

MARTIN, ROBERT, a merchant in Belfast, 1691. [RPCS.XVI.310]

MASH, RICHARD, 1694. [NAS.RH15.91.60]

MATHIE, JOHN, in Kilbryde, was alleged to have supplied weapons to the rebels in Ireland, 1601. [RPCS.V.324]

MATHY, JOHN, 1668. [NAS.RH15.91.60]

MATTHIE, JOHN, 1694. [NAS.RH15.91.60]

MAULE, THOMAS, a gentleman in St George's Lane, Dublin, 1659. [C]

MAXWELL, ANDREW, in Belfast, 1694. [NAS.RH15.91.60]

MAXWELL, COLIN, MD, in Londonderry, was admitted as a burgess and guilds-brother of Ayr on 3 September 1706. [ABR]

MAXWELL, GEORGE, in Sheeps Street, Dublin, 1659. [C]

MAXWELL, GEORGE, in Belfast, 8 November 1704, also 2 April 1709. [NAS.CH1/5/6/187, 190]

MAXWELL, JOHN, 1668. [NAS.RH15.91.60]

MAXWELL, JOHN, a seaman of Belfast, to be released from Edinburgh or Canongate Tolbooth in July 1689. [RPCS.XIII.554]

MAXWELL, PATRICK, in Ballikeill, leased Leasedrimbard, part of the townland of Altscale for 21 years from Milmore Ogneeve of Altscale, on 17 April 1641; a petitioner in 1651. [NAS.GD154.506/510]

MAXWELL, PATRICK, late in Lisdrumbard, 1651.
[NAS.GD154.510]

MAXWELL, Sir ROBERT, of Orchardton, in Ireland 1632.
[RPCS.IV.494]

MAXWELL, Sir ROBERT, a Protestant, fought under the Duke of
Hamilton, proprietor in the parish of Athlow, Barony of
Kennaght, County Londonderry, 1654. [CS]; of Ballycastle,
County Londonderry, 1664. [NAS.RH15.91.16]; resident in
Ireland 1668. [RPCS.II.436]

MAXWELL, Dr ROBERT, a Protestant and a proprietor in the
parish of Arbo, Barony of Dungannon, County Tyrone, 1654.
[CS]

MAXWELL, Sir ROBERT, Killyleagh, County Down, 1671, and
his wife Anne, 1684. [NAS.RH15.91.62]

MAXWELL, WILLIAM, of Steilstoun, allegedly transporting
stolen cattle to Ireland in 1626. [RPCS.I.421]

MAXWELL, Mrs, a widow, leased the townland of Balymoney,
parish of Dunboe, County Londonderry, on 4 September
1655. [NAS.RH15.91.59]

MEARS, JAMES, a merchant in Belfast, 1726. [NAS.AC9.967]

MILIKEN, JOHN, a merchant weaver in Ireland, was admitted as
a burgess and guilds-brother of Ayr on 1 July 1651. [ABR]

MILLER, ALEXANDER, tenant of 21 acres in Drumehoe, parish
of Kilwaghter, 1690, 1692, 1695.
[NAS.GD154.525/527/530/532]

MILLER, ANDREW, in Artikillie (?), 16... [NAS.RH15.91.49]

MILLER, HUGH, in the Barony of Glenarm, 1650s.
[NAS.GD154.512]

MILLAR, ..., in the Barony of Antrim, 1659. [C]

MITCHELBURN, ..., in Strangford, 1694. [NAS.RH15.91.60]

MITCHELL, GEORGE, in the Barony of Glenarm, 1650s. [NAS.GD154.512]

MITCHELL, JOHN, tenant in the 33 acres in the Barony of Glenarm, 1650s. [NAS.GD154.512/515]

MITCHELL, JOHN, in Artikillie, 16... [NAS.RH15.91.49]

MITCHELL, JOHN, a minister who fled from Ireland in 1689, settled in Ochiltree, Ayrshire, dead by 1691. [RPCS.XVI.517]

MITCHELL, ROBERT, in the Barony of Glenarm, 1650s. [NAS.GD154.512]

MOFFAT, HUGH, in Moneyreagh, County Down, 1671. [NAS.RH15.91.62

MOFFAT, THOMAS, lease of the townland of Gortieclaven, parish of Dunboe, County Londonderry, 9 April 1656. [NAS.RH15.91.59]

MOLLDUFF, MARION, a servant, 1694. [NAS.RH15.91.60]

MOLLMAN, JOHN, 1694. [NAS.RH15.91.60]

MONCREIFF, Lieutenant THOMAS, proprietor in the parish of Templecron, County Donegal, 1654. [CS]

MONCREIFF, THOMAS, a merchant in Diamond Street, Londonderry, 1659. [C]

MONEYPENNY, THOMAS, was granted the lands of Agalogha in the Barony of Knocknyny, County Fermanagh, on 13 August 1610. [TCD]

MONTEITH, JOHN, a merchant in Belfast, was admitted as a burgess and guilds-brother of Ayr on 29 August 1688. [ABR]

MONTGOMERIE, JANE, in the Bishops land in the parish of Ardstragh, Barony of Strabane, County Tyrone, 1654. [CS]

MONTGOMERIE, JOHN, in the Barony of Glenarm, 1650s.
[NAS.GD154.512/522]

MONTGOMERIE, MARY, in the Bishops land in the parish of
Ardstragh, Barony of Strabane, County Tyrone, 1654. [CS]

MONTGOMERIE, NINIAN, tenant in Leales and Drumnicho,
May 1645. [NAS.GD154.509]

MONTGOMERIE, ROBERT, in the Barony of Glenarm, 1650s.
[NAS.GD154.512]

MONTGOMERIE, THOMAS, in Irvine, was alleged to have
supplied weapons to the rebels in Ireland, 1601.
[RPCS.V.324]

MONTGOMERIE, WILLIAM, in the Barony of Glenarm, 1650s.
[NAS.GD154.512]

MONTGOMERIE, WILLIAM, a merchant in Dublin, was
admitted as a burgess and guilds-brother of Ayr on 17 July
1717. [ABR]

MONTGOMERY, ADAM, of Braidstone, an alleged pirate from
Ayr, was accused of looting the cargo on a ship of Thomas
Copran, a merchant in Dublin, off northern Ireland in 1586.
[RPCS.IV.72]

MONTGOMERY, ALEXANDER, in lands of Killoghtey, parish
of Killoghtey, County Donegal, 1654, by right of Katherine
Smith grandchild of John Smith of Boylestone. [CS]

MONTGOMERY, Sir HUGH, settled in Donaghadie during 1606.
[MM#51-67]

MONTGOMERY, HUGH, of the Braidstone family, arrived in
Ireland with Sir Hugh Montgomery in 1606, settled in
Donaghadie. [MM#51-67]

MONTGOMERY, HUGH, in County Fermanagh, with 500 acres,
11 men, 7 swords, 2 pikes, etc. [1641 Muster Roll of Ulster]

MONTGOMERY, HUGH, a Protestant and a proprietor in the

parish of Dunboe, Barony of Coleraine, County Londonderry, 1654. [CS]

MONTGOMERY, HUGH, a Protestant and a proprietor in the parish of Baltiagh, Barony of Kennaght, County Londonderry, 1654. [CS]

MONTGOMERY, HUGH, in Omagh, 1660-1670. [Hearth Money Rolls]

MONTGOMERY, HUGH, a merchant in Belfast, was admitted as a burgess and guilds-brother of Ayr on 11 July 1687. [ABR]

MONTGOMERY, JOHN, a gentleman in Corshendunyman, parish of Donoghmore, Barony of Rapho, County Donegal, 1659. [C]

MONTGOMERY, PATRICK, of Blackhouse, arrived in Ireland with Sir Hugh Montgomery in 1606, settled in Donaghadie. [MM#51-67]

MONTGOMERY, ROBERT, residing in Dublin 1585. [CBP.II.1227]

MONTGOMERY, ROBERT, in Archinlurchare, County Tyrone, 1612. [NAS.RH15.91.59]

MONTGOMERY, ROBERT, minister of the parish of Eregell, Barony of Coleraine, County Londonderry, pre 1641. [CS]

MONTGOMERY, ..., in the Barony of Antrim, 1659. [C]

MONTGOMERY, ..., in County Fermanagh, 1659. [C]

MOOR, ANDREW, tenant of 20 acres in Drumnahow, 1695. [NAS.GD154.532]

MOOR, CHARLES, in the Corbet, County Down, 1683. [NAS.GD10.828/830]

MOOR, GAVIN, in the Barony of Glenarm, 1650s. [NAS.GD154.512]

MOOR, JOHN, master of the <u>John of Hollywood</u>, arrived in Port Glasgow on 17 December 1689 from Belfast. [NAS.E72.19.1]

MOOR, JOHN, in the Barony of Glenarm, 1650s. [NAS.GD154.512]

MOOR, JOHN, son of John Moor a merchant in Dublin, was admitted as a burgess and guilds-brother of Ayr on 21 April 1726. [ABR]

MOORE, ROBERT, 1694. [NAS.RH15.91.60]

MORGAN, MARGARET, daughter of the late William Morgan, and wife of William Richardson, a farmer in Magharafelt, County Londonderry, 1694. [NAS.CC8.8.83/789]

MORGAN, Mrs MARGARET, widow of William Morgan, vicar of Arnugher, County West Meath, 1694. [NAS.CC8.8.83/789]

MORRILL, JAMES, in the Barony of Glenarm, 1650s. [NAS.GD154.512]

MORRIS, ROBERT, tenant of 10 acres in Belliderdawn, 1695. [NAS.GD154.532]

MORRISON, JAMES, 1668. [NAS.RH15.91.60]

MORTIMER, DAVID, a Protestant gentleman in Bellihursky, parish of Clandevadock, Barony of Killmaccrennan, County Donegal, 1654. [CS]; there in 1659. [C]

MORTIMER, WILLIAM, a Protestant gentleman in the parish of Clandevadock, Barony of Killmaccrennan, County Donegal, 1654. [CS]

MORTON, JOHN, in Irvine, was alleged to have supplied weapons to the rebels in Ireland, 1601. [RPCS.V.324]

MOSSMAN, JAMES, 1694. [NAS.RH15.91.60]

MOUAT, ANDREW, tenant of 20 acres in Drumahoe, parish of Kilwaghter, 1690. [NAS.GD154.525]

MOUTRAY, JOHN, a gentleman in Glencolmkill, parish of Killcarr, County Donegal, 1659. [C]

MOUTREA, JAMES, son of ….. Moutrea and his wife Anne Erskine, in County Tyrone around 1675. [NAS.RH9.17.103]

MOUTREA, MARY, daughter of ….. Moutrea and his wife Anne Erskine, in County Tyrone around 1675. [NAS.RH9.17.103]

MOWETT, ANDREW, leased the townlands of Kilvittee, Knocknocher and Bellybughtbegg, parish of Dunboe, County Londonderry, on 13 July 1655. [NAS.RH15.91.59]

MUIR, ADAM, tenant of 10 acres in Drumehoe, in the parish of Kilwaghter, 1690, 1692, 1695. [NAS.GD154.525/527/530/532]

MUIR, ANDREW, in Kilwaghter, 1690. [NAS.GD154.527/1]

MUIR, JAMES, in the Barony of Glenarm, 1650s. [NAS.GD154.512/515]

MUIR, JOHN, a merchant from Belfast, arrived in Port Glasgow on 1 January 1682 on the Ann of Belfast, master Robert Agnew. [NAS.E72.19.5]

MUIR, WILLIAM, of Glanderstone, authorised to transport horses from Ireland to Scotland on 10 November 1687. [RPCS.XIII.194]

MUIR, WILLIAM, tenant of 30 acres in the parish of Kilwaghter, 1690, 1692, 1693. [NAS.GD154.525/530/532]

MUIRHEAD, DAVID, 1694. [NAS.RH15.91.60]

MUIRHEAD, JOHN, 1668. [NAS.RH15.91.60]

MULHOLLAND, GEORGE, in the Barony of Glenarm, 1650s. [NAS.GD154.512]

MULLAN, JOHN, of Undergee, County Armagh, a soldier, to return from Scotland to Ireland in 1689. [RPCS.XIII.425]

MUNRO, HECTOR, an officer of the Danish Force in Ireland, 1689-1691. [DFI#146]

MURDOCH, JOHN, tenant of 2 acres in Lelish, parish of Kilwaghter, 1690. [NAS.GD154.525]

MURE, JOHN, a shipmaster in Kilbryde, was alleged to have supplied weapons to the rebels in Ireland, 1601. [RPCS.V.324]

MURE, JOHN, tenant in Drumnadonachie, May 1645. [NAS.GD154.509]

MURRAY, CHARLES, a gentleman in Drumbeg Balliboe, parish of Inver, Barony of Boylagh and Banagh, County Donegal, 1659. [C]

MURRAY, DAVID, leased the townland of Bellywolerikbeg, parish of Dunboe, County Londonderry, on 2 July 1655. [NAS.RH15.91.59]

MURRAY, GEORGE, of Broughton, was granted part of Boylaghe Eightra in the precinct of Boylaghe, County Donegal, on 9 September 1610. [TCD]

MURRAY, GEORGE, in Rathvily Barony, County Catherlagh, 1659. [C]

MURRAY, JAMES, in Inchkeill, Ireland, was serviced as heir to his father Alexander Murray of Blackcraig on 24 May 1670. [NAS.Retours]

MURRAY, JANET, moved to Ireland before 1659. [Mouswald KSR]

MURRAY, RICHARD, in Artikillie (?), 16... [NAS.RH15.91.49]

MURRAY, Sir ROBERT, of Glenmir, a gentleman in Castle Murray, parish of Killagtie, Barony of Boylagh and Banagh, County Donegal, 1659. [C]

MURRAY, WALTER, in the Barony of Rathvily, County Catherlagh, 1659. [C]

MURRAY, ..., in the Barony of Toome, County Antrim, 1659. [C]

NAISMITH, ALEXANDER, May 1702. [NAS.GD154.533/8]

NAPIER, JOHN, in the parish of Down, Barony of Lecale, County Down, 1659. [C]

NCINLEASTERE, MARIE, married Archibald McEuen in Ireland, and returned to Argyll, Scotland, by 1657. [RSA#2/162]

NCNICOLL, MOIRA, went from Argyll, Scotland, with Lachlan McNicoll, to marry in Ireland during 1653. [RSA#2/26]

NEAL, JAMES, in the Barony of Glenarm, 1650s. [NAS.GD154.512]

NEALSON, JAMES, 1707. [NAS.GD154.532]

NEILE, HENRY, a merchant in Pump Street, Londonderry, 1659. [C]

NEILSON, JAMES, son of John Neilson a cooper in Glasgow, was alleged to have supplied weapons to the rebels in Ireland, 1601. [RPCS.V.324]

NEILSON, JOHN, a cooper in Glasgow, was alleged to have supplied weapons to the rebels in Ireland, 1601. [RPCS.V.324]

NEILSON, ROBERT, Provost of Dungannon, justice of the peace for County Antrim, 1675. [NAS.RH9.17.103]

NEILSON, ROBERT, in Kilwaghter, 1690. [NAS.GD154.527/1]

NESBIT, ANDREW, a gentleman in the parish of Inver, Barony of Boylagh and Banagh, County Donegal, 1659. [C]

NESMITH, JAMES, a merchant in Pump Street, Londonderry, 1659. [C]

NEWPORT, DICK, a prisoner brought from Ireland to Scotland in 1690. [RPCS.XV.278]

NICHOLS, JAMES, in the Barony of Glenarm, 1650s. [NAS.GD154.512]

NICHOLS, JOHN, in the Barony of Glenarm, 1650s. [NAS.GD154.512]

NICOLSON, HUGH, born 1 November 1697, elder son of William Nicolson of Ballow, gentleman, and his wife Eleanor Dunlop, died 25 August 1722. [Bangor Old Church g/s]

NIGEL, MORRIS, in the Barony of Glenarm, 1650s. [NAS.GD154.512]

NISBET, ANDREW, in the Barony of Boylagh and Banagh, County Donegal, 1659. [C]

NISBET, ANDREW, a gentleman in Largimore, parish of Killcar, County Donegal, 1659. [C]

NISBET, JAMES, in Kilwaghter, 1690. [NAS.GD154.527/1]

NISBET, JOHN, a leasee in the parish of Rapho, County Donegal, 1654. [CS]

NISBET, Captain JOHN, in Tillidonell, parish of Rapho, Barony of Rapho, County Donegal, 1659. [C]

NISBET, JOHN, in Strabane, 1673. [NAS.GD10.447]

NISBET, ROBERT, 1694. [NAS.RH15.91.60]

NISBIT, JAMES, a gentleman in the parish of Inver, Barony of Boylagh and Banagh, County Donegal, 1659. [C]

NOBLE, WILLIAM, a gentleman in the parish of Taghboine, Barony of Rapho, County Donegal, 1659. [C]

NOBLE, ..., in County Fermanagh, 1659. [C]

NORMAN, CHARLES, in Londonderry, was admitted as a burgess and guilds-brother of Ayr on 3 September 1706. [ABR]

NOVELL, JAMES, a tenant in Lisdrumbard, 1651. [NAS.GD154.510]

NUGENT, RICHARD, an Irish corn-merchant in Ayr, 1599. [Ayr Burgh Accounts]

O'BRIAN, CORNELIUS, a prisoner brought from Ireland to Scotland in 1690. [RPCS.XV.278]

OCHILTREE, Lord, granted 3200 acres of Reuelinoutra in the precinct of Mountjoy, County Tyrone, on 9 April 1610. [TCD]

O'DONNALLY, QUENTIN, in Newton, Ireland, 10 January 1645. [NAS.CH1/5/4/27]

OGILVIE, GEORGE, a gentleman in Mylone, Barony of Belfast, County Antrim, 1659. [C]

OGILVIE, WILLIAM, minister in Larne, 1705, 1706. [NAS.GD154.532, 533/14]

ORR, WILLIAM, master of the <u>Ann of Donaghadie</u> at the port of Ayr on 14 February 1667. [NAS.E71.3.1]

OSBURN, ALEXANDER, 1694. [NAS.RH15.91.60]

OSBURN, HENRY, a merchant in Londonderry, eldest son of the late Henry Osburn, was admitted as a burgess and guilds-brother of Ayr on 7 April 1663. [ABR]

PAISLEY, JOHN, 1694. [NAS.RH15.91.60]

PARK, JOHN, tenant of 40 acres in the Barony of Glenarm, 1653. [NAS.GD154/515]

PATERSON, GAVEN, from County Down, a soldier, to return from Scotland to Ireland in 1689. [RPCS.XIII.425]

PATERSON, GAVEN, 1694. [NAS.RH15.91.60]

PATERSON, ROBERT, 1694. [NAS.RH15.91.60]

PATERSON, WILLIAM, in Artikillie , 16... [NAS.RH15.91.49]

PATON, JOHN, a gentleman in Ballyriskbeg, Barony of Kenaght, County Londonderry, 1659. [C]

PATTERSON, HANNIBAL, a leasee in the parish of Rapho, County Donegal, 1654. [CS]

PATTERSON, JOHN, from County Down, a soldier, to return from Scotland to Ireland in 1689. [RPCS.XIII.425]

PATTERSON, ROBERT, 1674. [NAS.RH15.91.60]

PATTERSON, WILLIAM, 1668. [NAS.RH15.91.60]

PATTON, ELISE, widow of David McCullogh, leasee in the parish of Tulloghobegly, Barony of Killmacrennan, County Donegal, 1654. [CS]

PATTON, HENRY, a Protestant gentleman in the parish of Clandevadock, Barony of Killnaccrenan, County Donegal, 1654. [CS]; there in 1659, [C]

PATTON, JOHN, 1694. [NAS.RH15.91.60]

PATTON, WILLIAM, a Protestant and a clerk, a proprietor in the parish of Clandevadock, Barony of Killmacrennan, County Donegal, dead by 1654. [CS]

PEACOCK, PATRICK, a Presbyterian minister in northern Ireland, 1679. [RPCS.VI.657]

PEARSON, ARCHIBALD, a gentleman in the parish of Killagtie, Barony of Boylagh and Banagh, County Donegal, 1659. [C]

PEEBLES, HUGH, tenant of 16 acres in the Barony of Glenarm, 1650s. [NAS.GD154.512/515]

PEEBLES, JOHN, (1), in the Barony of Glenarm, 1650s. [NAS.GD154.512]

PEEBLES, JOHN, (2), in the Barony of Glenarm, 1650s. [NAS.GD154.512/515]

PETTICREW, WILLIAM, 1694. [NAS.RH15.91.60]

PETTYCROVE, GAVIN, a servant of William Hamilton of Killeach in Ireland, was admitted as a burgess and guilds-brother of Ayr on 25 September 1699. [ABR]

PHILLIPS, JANE, widow of Robert Hamilton of Belliferris, a merchant in Killileach, County Down, fled with her husband to Scotland in 1689. [RPCS.XIII.448]

PHILLIPS, THOMAS, Governor of Londonderry, reference in document with no date but after 1613. [NAS.RH9.17.32/1]

PHILP, GILBERT, a trooper in the Earl of Eglinton's troop in Ireland, 1690. [RPCS.XV.220]

PHILP, JAMES, an undertaker in County Longford, 1621. [RPCS.XII.420]

PILLMAN, (?), THOMAS, tenant of 5 acres in the Barony of Glenarm, 1650s. [NAS.GD154.512/515/525]

PILSWORTH, ROBERT, murdered Mr Alexander Burrows in Ireland during 1636. [RPCS.VI.279]

PIRIE, JOHN, a Protestant refugee from Ireland, in Edinburgh 1689. [RPCS.XIII.410]

PITCAIRN, JEAN, in Artikillie (?), 16... [NAS.RH15.91.49]

PITTILOW, JOHN, master of the bark Sarah of Coleraine arrived in Port Glasgow on 2 June 1681 from Londonderry. [NAS.E71.19.1]

POACK, GEORGE, of Killileach, County Down, a soldier, to return from Scotland to Ireland in 1689. [RPCS.XIII.425]

POLLOCK, ANNA, relict of Andrew Mitchell in Kilbridie, Ireland, and Agnes Pollock, relict of Adam Galt in Grange of Kildalloch, Balrishean parish, Ireland, heirs to their brother James Pollock a messenger in Maybole, 28 October 1698.[NAS.GD25.Sec7/110]

POLLOCK, GEORGE, in Glasgow, was alleged to have supplied weapons to the rebels in Ireland, 1601. [RPCS.V.324]

PONT, MARTHA, widow of Reverend Josias Pont in Templepatrick, Ireland, and their children John, Margaret, and Lucy, 1656. [NAS,RD{C&S} 585/19]

PORTER, HEW, a former burgess of Irvine, Ayrshire, settled at Lochlerne, Ireland, before 1665. [Irvine Council Book, 26.5.1665]

PORTER, JAMES, son of Hew Porter in Lochlerne, Ireland, was admitted as a burgess of Irvine, Ayrshire, Scotland, on 26 May 1665. [Irvine Council Book]

POTTER, THOMAS, 1694. [NAS.RH15.91.60]

POTTINGER, Captain EDWARD, a merchant in Belfast, was admitted as a burgess and guilds-brother of Ayr on 28 August 1689. [ABR]

RAMSAY, ELIZABETH, in Mouswald parish, Dumfries-shire, in 1656, formerly in Ireland. [Mouswald KSR, 20.4.1656]

RAMSAY, GILBERT, member of the Presbytery of Bangor, 27 September 1649. [NAS.CH1/5/4/59]

RAMSAY, JAMES, in the Barony of Glenarm, 1650s. [NAS.GD154.512]

RAMSAY, JAMES, tenant of 37 acres in Drumadonachan, parish of Kilwaghter, 1690, 1693. [NAS.GD154.525, 527, 529]

RANKINE, JAMES, in Irvine, was alleged to have supplied weapons to the rebels in Ireland, 1601. [RPCS.V.324]

RANKINE, JOHN, in Irvine, was alleged to have supplied weapons to the rebels in Ireland, 1601. [RPCS.V.324]

RANKINE, JOHN, in Kildrum, County Antrim, son and heir of William Rankine in Auldmur, Ayrshire, 1677. [NAS.SH.25.4.1677]

RANKINE, WILLIAM, a Protestant and leasee in the parish of Rapho, County Donegal, 1654. [CS]

RANKINE, WILLIAM, master of the Catherine of Larne, from Port Glasgow to Belfast on 31 January 1681. [NAS.E72.19.2]

READ, ALEXANDER, of Ardekelly, County Londonderry, 1664. [NAS.RH15.91.16]

REID, ALEXANDER, in Artikillie, 1695. [NAS.RH15.91.49]

REID, ALEXANDER, master of the Jane of Hollywood from Port Glasgow to Belfast on 31 January 1681. [NAS.E72.19.2]

REID, DAVID, nephew of Gilbert Thomson a burgess of Ayr, was murdered on the 'Isle of Rachrie' in September 1584. [RPCS.V.393]

REID, JAMES, a seaman of Belfast, to be released from Edinburgh or Canongate Tolbooth in July 1689. [RPCS.XIII.554]

REID, JAMES, in Kilwaghter, 1690. [NAS.GD154.527/1]

REID, JOHN, a smith in Donachadie, 1677, lease of lands of Auchtifie for 19 years from 1690. [NAS.GD154.441]

REID, THOMAS, in Meochill, parish of Achadowy, County Londonderry, and his wife Katherine Wyllie, contract with Hugh Thompson, a flesher burgess of Irvine, Ayrehisre, 14 August 1665, and 8 December 1665. [NAS.GD1/693/11, 12]

REID, UCHTRED, brother of John Reid a smith in Donachadie, 1677, lease of lands of Auchtifie for 19 years from 1690. [NAS.GD154.441]

REID, WALTER, in the Barony of Glenarm, 1650s, a tenant in the parish of Kilwaghter, 1660s. [NAS.GD154.512/525]

REID, WILLIAM, an Irishman and former soldier, guilty of murder in Angus in 1654. [RPCS.I.251]

REID, WILLIAM, of Daldilling, Ayrshire, a minister in Ireland, who died before 1691, father of William. [NAS.SH.8.9.1691]

REID, ..., in the Barony of Belfast, County Antrim, 1659. [C]

RICHARD, JAMES, arrived in Scotland from Ireland and imprisoned as a suspected rebel, 1686. [RPCS.XII.324]

RICHARDSON, ALEXANDER, a Protestant and proprietor in the parish of Killdress, Barony of Dungannon, County Tyrone, 1654. [CS]

RICHARDSON, ALEXANDER, in County Tyrone, 1675. [NAS.RH9.17.103]

RICHARDSON, ARCHIBALD, in Augher, County Tyrone, 1707. [NAS.GD112.15.729]

RICHARDSON, JAMES, at the Siege of Londonderry, 1689. [NAS.GD112.15.729]

RICHARDSON, WILLIAM, a minister in Killileoch, was admitted as a burgess and guilds-brother of Ayr on 18 October 1661, through the right of his wife daughter of John Osburn late Provost of Ayr. [ABR]

RICHARDSON, W., member of the Presbytery of Bangor, 27 September 1649. [NAS.CH1/5/4/59]

RICHIE, JOHN, in Artikillie, 1695 [NAS.RH15.91.49]

ROBERTS, EDWARD, 1668. [NAS.RH15.91.60]

ROBERTSON, JOHN, a Protestant and a proprietor in the parish of Artrea, Barony of Dungannon, County Tyrone, dead by 1654. [CS]

ROBINS, THOMAS, a merchant in Dublin, was admitted as a burgess and guilds-brother of Glasgow on 13 January 1724. [BRG]

RODGER, JAMES, a merchant in Londonderry, 1663. [NAS.GD8.1663]

RODGER, JOHN, master of the James of Larne at the port of Ayr on 25 February 1667. [NAS.E71.3.1]

RODGERS, ROBERT, of County Armagh, a soldier, to return from Scotland to Ireland in 1689. [RPCS.XIII.425]

ROSE, ROBERT, in Kilwaghter, 1690. [NAS.GD154.527/1]

ROSS, ALEXANDER, in the Barony of Glenarm, 1650s. [NAS.GD154.512]

ROSS, ALEXANDER, moved from Islay, Argyll, to Insch, Derry, Ireland, in 1657. [RSA#2/144]

ROSS, JAMES, tenant of 8 acres in Belliadordanon, in the parish of Kilwaghter, 1690, 1692, 1695. [NAS.GD154.525/530/532]

ROSS, JOHN, in Glasgow, was alleged to have supplied weapons to the rebels in Ireland, 1601. [RPCS.V.324]

ROSS, JOHN, in the Barony of Glenarm, 1650s. [NAS.GD154.512]

ROSS, JOHN, tenant of 8 acres in Belliadordanon, parish of Kilwaghter, 1690, 1692. [NAS.GD154.525/530]

ROSS, ROBERT, tenant of 10 acres in Drumahoe, parish of Kilwaghter, 1690. [NAS.GD154.525]

ROSS, WILLIAM, leased the townland of Dingonie, parish of Dunboe, County Londonderry, on 30 June 1655. [NAS.RH15.91.59]

ROSS, the widow, tenant of 10 acres in Drumahoe, 1695.
[NAS.GD154.532]

ROUGTON, ISABEL, in Artikillie (?), 16… [NAS.RH15.91.49]

ROWAN, Captain WILLIAM, to Ireland with soldiers in 1689.
[RPCS.XIII.459]

RUSH, JASPER, a prisoner brought from Ireland to Scotland in
1690. [RPCS.XV.278]

RUSSELL, ALEXANDER, in the Barony of Glenarm, 1650s.
[NAS.GD154.512]

RUSSELL, JOHN, a prisoner brought from Ireland to Scotland in
1690. [RPCS.XV.278]

RUSSELL, ROBERT, tenant of 30 acres in the parish of
Kilwaghter, 1660s. [NAS.GD154.525.2/2]

RUTHERFORD, JAMES, 1673. [NAS.RH15.91.60]

SANDERSON, ARCHIBALD, a Protestant and a proprietor in the
parish of Dissertereagh, Barony of Dungannon, County
Tyrone, dead by 1654. [CS]

SANDERSON, Colonel ROBERT, in Belligrugan, parish of
Derrygloran, Barony of Dungannon, also a proprietor in the
parish of Dissertereagh, County Tyrone, 1654. [CS]

SANDERSON, Captain, an undertaker in County Tyrone, with
1000 acres, 34 men, 18 swords, 9 pikes, etc. [1641 Muster
Roll of Ulster]

SANDS, JAMES, in the Barony of Glenarm, 1650s.
[NAS.GD154.512]

SANDS, WILLIAM, in Gallen Barony, Meelick parish, County
Mayo. [BSD, 1636-1703]

SCALLAN, JAMES, a prisoner brought from Ireland to Scotland
in 1690. [RPCS.XV.278]

SCOTT, HUGH, born 1705, a minister, died 26 March 1736.
[Donegore g/s, County Antrim]

SCOTT, JAMES, in Artikillie, 1695 [NAS.RH15.91.49]

SCOTT, JOHN, in Artikillie, 1695 [NAS.RH15.91.49]

SCOTT, THOMAS, master of the Content of Balliwater and owner
of the Content of Belfast, at the port of Ayr in 1676.
[RPCS.III.583]

SCOTT, THOMAS, in Artikillie (?), 16... [NAS.RH15.91.49]

SCOTT, WILLIAM, in the Barony of Ballyadams, Queen's
County, 1659. [C]

SCOTT, ..., in the Barony of Boylagh and Banagh, County
Donegal, 1659. [C]

SCOTT, ..., in County Fermanagh, 1659. [C]

SEAWRIGHT, JOHN, in Kilwaghter, 1690. [NAS.GD154.527/1]

SEEDS, WILLIAM, born 1679, a merchant in Belfast, died on 13
November 1746. [Derriaghy g/s, County Antrim]

SEMPEL, THOMAS, in Kilwaghter, 1690. [NAS.GD154.527/1]

SEMPILL, BRYCE, of Cathcart, bound over for the assise of
County Londonderry in 1631. [RPCS.IV.154]

SEMPILL, LEVINIS, a gentleman in Letterkenny town, parish of
Conwall, Barony of Killmccrenan, County Donegal, 1659.
[C]

SEMPILL, Sir WILLIAM, a Protestant and leasee in the parish of
Lecke, County Donegal, 1654. [CS]

SEMPLE, ALEXANDER, a Protestant and a leasee in Bishops
Lands in Capella of Littermcaward, County Donegal, 1654.
[CS]

SEMPLE, DUNCAN, master of the <u>Antelope of Glasgow</u> in Tyrconnel 1608. [RPCS.III.205]

SEMPLE, W., in Dublin, March 1671. [NAS.CH1/5/6/124-125]

SEMPLE, WILLIAM, a cleric in the parish of Conwall, Barony of Killmaccrenan, County Donegal, 1654. [CS]

SERVICE, WILLIAM, tenant of 20 acres in the Barony of Glenarm, 1650s. [NAS.GD154.512/515]

SETON, JOHN, an officer of the Danish Force in Ireland, 1689-1691. [DFI#146]

SHARPE, JAMES, tenant of 20 acres in the parish of Kilwaghter, 1690, 1692, 1693, 1695. [NAS.GD154.525/530/532]

SHAW, JAMES, of Bellygelly, 1654. [NAS.GD153.517]; in Bellygelly, parish of Carncastle, County Antrim, 1659. [C]

SHAW, JAMES, minister of Carmonie in Ireland, by right of his wife Margaret, second daughter of Robert Gordon the late Provost of Ayr and his wife Susanna Kennedy, was admitted as a burgess and guilds-brother of Ayr on 15 June 1658. [APR]

SHAW, JAMES, in the Barony of Glenarm, 1650s. [NAS.GD154.512]

SHAW, JOHN, of Greenock, arrived in Ireland with Sir Hugh Montgomery in 1606, settled in Donaghadie. [MM#51-67]

SHAW, Captain, JOHN, in the Barony of Glenarm, 1650s. [NAS.GD154.512]

SHAW, JOHN, a gentleman in Cairnfinock, parish of Carncastle, County Antrim, 1659. [C]

SHAW, JOHN, son of James Shaw of Bellygelly, parish of Carncastle, County Antrim, 1659. [C]

SHAW, LANCELOT, in the Barony of Glenarm, 1650s. [NAS.GD154.512]

SHAW, PATRICK, of Kelsoland, arrived in Ireland with Sir Hugh Montgomery in 1606, settled in Donaghadie. [MM#51-67]

SHAW, PATRICK, 1702. [NAS.GD154.532]

SHAW, WILLIAM, a gentleman in Moylmey, Barony of Antrim, 1659. [C]

SHAW, WILLIAM, of Bush Edge, Kilwaghter (?), 1695, 1696, 1702. [NAS.GD154.533/1, 2, 9]

SHAW, W., in Newton, Ireland, 10 January 1645. [NAS.CH1/5/4/27]

SHAW, the widow, in the Barony of Glenarm, 1650s. [NAS.GD154.512]

SHEARER, DAVID, in Glasgow, was alleged to have supplied weapons to the rebels in Ireland, 1601. [RPCS.V.324]

SHEARER, JAMES, master of the doggar The Matthew of Belfast, was admitted as a burgess and guilds-brother of Ayr on 22 June 1725. [ABR]

SHEARER, JAMES, master of the Batchelor of Belfast, from Scotland to Stockholm, Sweden, in 1729. [NAS.E502]

SHEARER, THOMAS, a seaman of Belfast, to be released from Edinburgh or Canongate Tolbooth in July 1689. [RPCS.XIII.554]

SHENNAN, JOHN, 1694. [NAS.RH15.91.60]

SHEPHERD, EDWARD, in Artikillie, 16... [NAS.RH15.91.49]

SHIELL, JOHN, a tenant in the parish of Kilwaghter, 1692. [NAS.GD154.530]

SIME, JAMES, a gentleman in Magherireagh, parish of Donoghmore, Barony of Rapho, County Donegal, 1659. [C]

SIME, JOHN, son of James Sime, a gentleman in Magherireagh, parish of Donoghmore, Barony of Rapho, County Donegal, 1659. [C]

SIMSON, WILLIAM, in Glasgow, was alleged to have supplied weapons to the rebels in Ireland, 1601. [RPCS.V.324]

SINCLAIR, Sir WILLIAM, an undertaker in County Longford, 1621. [RPCS.XII.420]

SINCLAIR, WILLIAM, born 1679, a merchant in Belfast, died 24 December 1759, husband of (1) Jane Gregg (1682-1714), and (2) Jane Scott (1685-1760). [Belfast g/s]

SMAILHOLM, GEORGE, was granted the lands of Dirrianny in the Barony of Knocknyny, County Fermanagh, on 13 August 1610. [TCD]

SMAILLIE, WILLIAM, in Lochlairne, Antrim, 1628. [NAS.RS.Ayr#2/230-232]

SMALLET, JOHN, apprentice to Gideon Murray a merchant burgess of Edinburgh, a thief who absconded to Ireland in 1655. [RPCS.I.200]

SMITH, JOHN, a Protestant and leasee in the parish of Rapho, County Donegal, 1654. [CS]

SMITH, JOHN, merchant on the Elizabeth of Larne at the port of Ayr on 22 May 1678. [NAS.E72.3.4]

SMITH, Reverend JOHN, returning from Scotland to Clocher, County Tyrone, in 1690. [RPCS.XV.302]

SMITH, ROBERT, tenant of 8 acres in Belliderdawn, 1695. [NAS.GD154.532]

SMITH, THOMAS, servant of John Hunter rector of Bonvery in Ireland, was admitted as a burgess and guilds-brother of Ayr on 8 November 1692. [ABR]

SMITH, THOMAS, born 1662, died 20 August 1733. [Armoy g/s, County Antrim]

SOANWRIGHT, JOHN, tenant of 12 acres in Drumnadonachan, parish of Kilwaghter, 1690. [NAS.GD154.525]

SOMERVILL, WILLIAM, a barber in Dublin, was admitted as a burgess and guilds-brother of Glasgow on 1 August 1717. [BRG]

SPEIR, JOHN, tenant of 10 acres in Drumahow, parish of Kilwaghter, 1690, 1691, 1692, 1695. [NAS.GD154.525/528/530/532]

SPOTSWOOD, ANNE, heiress of Dr James Spotswood, a leasee in the parish of Lifford, County Donegal, 1654. [CS]

SPOTSWOOD, ELIZABETH, heiress of Dr James Spotswood, a leasee in the parish of Lifford, County Donegal, 1654. [CS]

SPOTSWOOD, Sir HENRY, a leasee in the parish of Clogher, County Tyrone, 1654. [CS]

SPOTSWOOD, Dr JAMES, leased lands in the parish of Lifford, County Donegal, from Dr John Bromhill then Bishop of Derry, in 1634. [CS]

SPROULE, ARCHIBALD, a Protestant and a leasee in the parish of Rapho, County Donegal, 1654, which he bought from his brother Robert Sproule and Alexander Innes, which they obtained from Dr John Lesly the Bishop of Rapho. [CS]; in Boggagh and Stranorlaghan, parish of Rapho, 1659. [C]

SPROULE, JOHN, a gentleman in Boggagh and Stranorlaghan, parish of Rapho, Barony of Rapho, County Donegal, 1659. [C]

STEILL, GAVEN, a gentleman in the parish of Roscarken, County Antrim, 1659. [C]

STEILL, JOHN, senior, in the Barony of Glenarm, 1650s. [NAS.GD154.512]

STEILL, JOHN, tenant of 6 acres in the Barony of Glenarm, 1650s. [NAS.GD154.512/515]

STEILL, JOHN, tenant of 8 acres in Drumnadonachan, parish of
Kilwaghter, 1690, 1692, 1695.
[NAS.GD154.525/527/530/532]

STEILL, THOMAS, tenant in Drumnadonachie, May 1645.
[NAS.GD154.509]

STEIN, JOHN tenant of 45 acres in the parish of Kilwaghter, 1690,
1692. [NAS.GD154.525/530]

STEVENS, HUMPHREY, from County Armagh, a soldier, to
return from Scotland to Ireland in 1689. [RPCS.XIII.425]

STEWART, ALEXANDER, an undertaker in County Donegal,
with 1000 acres, 32 men, 17 swords, 9 pikes, 1 muskets, etc.
[1641 Muster Roll of Ulster]

STEWART, Sir ALEXANDER, a Protestant and a proprietor in
Mountstewart, parish of Clogher, Barony of Clogher, County
Tyrone, 1654. [CS]

STEWART, Sir ALEXANDER, proprietor of Carrick Abbey,
parish of Bodony, Barony of Strabane, lands in the parish of
Ardstragh and in the parish of Cappy, County Tyrone, dead
by 1654, heir to Sir William Stewart. [CS]

STEWART, ALEXANDER, a Protestant gentleman in
Downdowanmore, parish of Mevagh, Barony of
Killmaccrenan, County Donegal, 1654. [CS]

STEWART, ALEXANDER, a gentleman in Drumnert, the parish
of Bellemone, County Antrim, 1659. [C]

STEWART, ALEXANDER, in Ballimore, parish of Clandehurka,
Barony of Killmccrenan, County Donegal, 1659. [C]

STEWART, Sir ANDREW, an undertaker in County Tyrone, with
4500 acres, 93 men, 86 swords, 45 pikes, etc. [1641 Muster
Roll of Ulster]

STEWART, ANDREW, a Protestant and proprietor of Ardcomer, parishes of Deryloran, and of Dissertereagh, Barony of Dungannon, County Tyrone, 1654. [CS]

STEWART, ANDREW, in Morris, parish of Templemore, Barony of Enishowen, County Donegal, 1659. [C]

STEWART, DAVID, a Protestant, residing in Killconnell, parish of Killmacrennan, County Donegal, 1654. [CS]; there in 1658. [C]

STEWART, FRANCIS, son of John Stewart, a gentleman in Drumoghell, parish of Ray, Barony of Rapho, County Donegal, 1659. [C]

STEWART, HARRY, brought from Ireland as a prisoner and imprisoned in Edinburgh Tolbooth in 1665. [RPCS.II.111]

STEWART, HENRY, an undertaker in County Tyrone, with 1500 acres, 46 men, 27 swords, 7 pikes, 3 muskets, etc. [1641 Muster Roll of Ulster]

STEWART, HENRY, a Protestant and a proprietor in the parish of Killamen, Barony of Dungannon, County Tyrone, 1654. [CS]

STEWART, JAMES, a Protestant and a proprietor in the parish of Donaghenry, Barony of Dungannon, County Tyrone, 1654. [CS]

STEWART, JAMES, a Protestant and a proprietor in the parish of Derrygloran, Barony of Dungannon, County Tyrone, 1654. [CS]

STEWART, JAMES, a gentleman in Mondowy, parish of Ray, Barony of Rapho, County Donegal, 1659. [C]

STEWART, Captain JAMES, of Killinare, 1702. [NAS.GD154.534]

STEWART, Sir JOHN, of Methven, in Ireland, 1627. [RPCS.II.xv]

STEWART, JOHN, an undertaker in County Donegal, with 1000 acres, 13 men, 8 swords, 1 pike, etc. [1641 Muster Roll of Ulster]

STEWART, Captain JOHN, a leasee in the parish of Ray, County Donegal, 1654. [CS]

STEWART, JOHN, a gentleman in Cowlglee, parish of Ray, Barony of Rapho, County Donegal, 1659. [C]

STEWART, JOHN, a gentleman in Drumoghell, parish of Ray, Barony of Rapho, County Donegal, 1659. [C]

STEWART, Major JOHN, returned from Ireland to Dunduff in 1665. [RPCS.II.74]

STEWART, JOHN, of Bellidraine, born 1621, died 4 November 1691. [Drumbeg g/s]

STEWART, JOHN, a gentleman in the parish of Bellemone, County Antrim, 1659. [C]

STEWART, Lady KATHERINE, and her son **Sir WILLIAM STEWART** a minor, Protestants and proprietors in the parish of Aghneish, Barony of Killmacrenan, County Donegal, 1654. [CS]

STEWART, MATTHEW, a gentleman in Drumbarn, parish of Ray, Barony of Rapho, County Donegal, 1659. [C]

STEWART, PATRICK, tenant of 10 acres in the parish of Kilwaghter, 1690, 1692. [NAS.GD154.525/527/530]

STEWART, ROBERT, was recommended by the Synod of Argyll to the Presbytery of Knockfergus, Ireland, on 5 July 1645. [RSA#1/95]

STEWART, Lieutenant Colonel ROBERT, a Protestant and a proprietor in the parish of Donagheny, Barony of Dungannon, County Tyrone, 1654. [CS]

STEWART, ROBERT, a gentleman in the parish of Bellemone, County Antrim, 1659. [C]

STEWART, ROBERT, a gentleman in Cowlglee, parish of Ray, Barony of Rapho, County Donegal, 1659. [C]

STEWART, SAMUEL, a minister who fled from Ireland in 1689, settled in Girvan, [RPCS.XVI.256]

STEWART, THOMAS, a Protestant and proprietor in the parish of Conwall, County Donegal, 1654, son of the late Sir William Stewart. [CS]

STEWART, THOMAS, a Protestant and proprietor in the parishes of Aghneish, Barony of Aghneish, and of Tully, Barony of Killmaccrenan, County Donegal, 1654. [CS]; there in 1659, [C]

STEWART, Captain THOMAS, in Magherhy, parish of Drumhome, Barony of Tirhugh, County Donegal, 1659. [C]

STEWART, THOMAS, a land laborer from Balneculhom, County Donegal, with his wife and children, sailed from there to Saltcoats in Scotland in 1686. [RPCS.XII.379]

STEWART, THOMAS, 1694. [NAS.RH15.91.60]

STEWART, THOMAS, in Artikillie, 1695 [NAS.RH15.91.49]

STEWART, Captain WILLIAM, sent to Carrickfergus, Ireland, with 200 soldiers in June 1608. [RPCS.VIII.511]

STEWART, WILLIAM, was granted the lands of Downcanally in the Barony of Boylaghe, County Donegal, on 9 September 1610. [TCD]

STEWART, WILLIAM, of Dunduff, was granted part of Cooleaghie in the Barony of Portloghe, County Donegal, on 26 September 1610. [TCD]

STEWART, Sir WILLIAM, an undertaker in County Tyrone, with 4000 acres, 130 men, 64 swords, 32 pikes, 7 muskets, etc. [1641 Muster Roll of Ulster]

STEWART, WILLIAM, a Protestant, a leasee in the parish of
Taboyne, County Donegal, 1654, held in inheritance from his
father and grandfather. [CS]

STEWART, WILLIAM, a Protestant and a leasee in the parish of
Ray, County Donegal, 1654. [CS]

STEWART, WILLIAM, in Bellilane, parish of Ray, Barony of
Rapho, County Donegal, 1659. [C]

STEWART, ..., of Dunduff, an undertaker in County Donegal,
with 1000 acres, 61 men, 44 swords, 14 pikes, 1 muskets, etc.
[1641 Muster Roll of Ulster]

STEWART, Captain, 1694. [NAS.RH15.91.60]

STIRLING, Sir ROBERT, in the parish of Atherdee, Drogheda,
1659. [C]

STOKER, ANNA, a widow in Belfast, 1687. [NAS.CC8.8.78/512]

STORMONT, Lord THOMAS, in Belliwell, parish of Killamarde,
Barony of Boylagh and Banagh, County Donegal, 1659. [C]

STOTSWOOD, M., 1694. [NAS.RH15.91.60]

STUART, ANDREW, member of the Presbytery of Bangor, 27
September 1649. [NAS.CH1/5/4/59]

STUART, ANDREW, a gentleman in Ballymcegan, parish of
Lorha, County Tipperary, 1659. [C]

STUART, ARCHIBALD, a gentleman in Ballantoy, parish of
Billy, County Antrim, 1659. [C]

STUART, Lieutenant Colonel WALTER, in the Lyne of
Mounterady, Barony of Toome, County Antrim, 1659. [C]

STUART, WILLIAM, a gentleman in Ridbay, parish of Lays,
County Antrim, 1659. [C]

STUART, ..., in the Barony of Toome, County Antrim, 1659. [C]

SYMSON, WILLIAM, master of the <u>William of Hollywood,</u> arrived in Port Glasgow on 2 June 1681 from Belfast. [NAS.E72.19.1]

TAGGART, ..., in the Barony of Antrim, 1659. [C]

TAIT, PATRICK, a leasee in the parish of Belliclogg, Barony of Dungannon, County Tyrone, from 1630. [CS]

TARBERT, THOMAS, in the Barony of Glenarm, 1650s. [NAS.GD154.512]

TAYLOR, EUPHAN, a debtor in 1702. [NAS.GD154.532]

TENNAND, JOHN, a merchant, was admitted as a burgess and guilds-brother of Ayr on 22 June 1700, through the right of his wife Susanna daughter of the late Reverend James Shaw in Carmonie, Ireland. [ABR]

THOMSON, ANTHONY, son of Archibald Thomson, a gentleman in Galdinagh, parish of Ray, Barony of Rapho, County Donegal, 1659. [C]

THOMSON, ARCHIBALD, in Ballibegly, parish of Taboyne, County Donegal, 1654. [CS]

THOMSON, ARCHIBALD, gentleman in Galdinagh, parish of Ray, County Donegal, 1654. [CS], and there in 1659. [C]

THOMSON, CHARLES, master of the <u>Providence of Larne</u> from Ayr to Dublin on 3 November 1690. [NAS.E72.3.27]

THOMSON, GEORGE, son of Hugh Thomson a merchant in Londonderry, sold lands in the parish of Ray, County Donegal, before 1654. [CS]

THOMSON, GILBERT, a burgess of Ayr, trading to Loch Foyle in September 1584. [RPCS.V.393]

THOMSON, HENRY, a Protestant and proprietor of Gortergerties, parish of Faughanvale, Barony of Terkerin, County Londonderry, 1654. [CS]

THOMSON, HUGH, a merchant in Londonderry, and his wife Elizabeth Erskine, 1621. [NAS.RS.Argyll#1/139]

THOMSON, HUGH, in Altaghaderry, parish of Taboyne, County Donegal, 1654. [CS]

THOMSON, HUGH, a Protestant gentleman in the parish of Clandevadock, County Donegal, 1654. [CS]

THOMSON, HUGH, a merchant in Pump Street, Londonderry, 1659. [C]

THOMSON, JANET, 1694. [NAS.RH15.91.60]

THOMSON, JOHN, a cleric, in the parish of Clandehurka, Barony of Killmacrennan, County Donegal, 1654. [CS]

THOMSON, JOHN, moved from Argyll, Scotland, to Ireland in 1657. [RSA#2/145]

THOMSON, JOHN, son of Archibald Thomson, a gentleman in Galdinagh, parish of Ray, Barony of Rapho, County Donegal, 1659. [C]

THOMSON, JOHN, the elder, a merchant in Coleraine, and Hugh Thomson, a flesher burgess of Irvine, Ayrshire, 8 June 1688. [NAS.GD1/693/16]

THOMSON, JOHN, of Sevenacres, a merchant in Coleraine, son and heir of John Thomson, the elder, a merchant in Coleraine, sasine in favour of George Craig, merchant in Irvine, and his wife Margaret Glasgow, 14 March 1711, and 14 March 1715. [NAS.GD1/693/19, 20]

THOMSON, LOUIS, a merchant in Belfast, 1691. [RPCS.XVI.309]

THOMSON, ROBERT, in the Barony of Glenarm, 1650s. [NAS.GD154.512]

THOMSON, ROBERT, in Kilwaghter, 1690. [NAS.GD154.527/1]

THOMSON, WALTER, master of the James of Donaghadie at Dumfries on 3 May 1691. [NAS.E72.6.22]

THOMSON, the widow, 1694. [NAS.RH15.91.60]

THOMSON, WILLIAM, leased the townland of Ballymoney, parish of Dunboe, County Londonderry, on 4 September 1655. [NAS.RH15.91.59]

THOMSON, WILLIAM, tenant of 10 acres in Lelish, parish of Kilwaghter, 1690, 1692. [NAS.GD154.525/527/530]

THOMPSON, WILLIAM, tenant of 30 acres in the Barony of Glenarm, 1650s. [NAS.GD154.512/515]

TRUMBLE, GEORGE, in the Barony of Glenarm, 1650s. [NAS.GD154.512]

TRUMBLE, JOHN, in the Barony of Glenarm, 1650s. [NAS.GD154.512]

TRUMBLE, WILLIAM, in the Barony of Glenarm, 1650s. [NAS.GD154.512]

TURNBULL, DAVID, a gentleman in Graignakent, parish of Knockgraffon, Barony of Middlethird, County Tipperary, 1659. [C]

TURNBULL, MATHEW, in Glasgow, was alleged to have supplied weapons to the rebels in Ireland, 1601. [RPCS.V.324]

TWEED, ARCHIBALD, of Drumain, born 1687, died 19 February 1800, and his wife Jane, born 1713, died on 17 December 1815. [Carncastle g/s, County Antrim]

TWEED, JOHN, born 1647, died 2 February 1719. [Carncastle g/s, County Antrim]

TWEED, ROBERT, born 1670, husband of Margaret Young, died on 11 December 1759. [Carncastle g/s, County Antrim]

VALLANGE, JAMES, of Possil, married Barbara Fullerton, Lady
Freuch, at Newton of Clonnis Cowers, Ireland, around 1687.
[NAS.CC8.Consistorial Processes, 3 May 1707]

VANCE, PATRICK, of Layebrick, was granted part of Boylaghe
Outraghe in the precinct of Boylaghe, County Donegal, on 9
September 1610. [TCD]

VANS, WILLIAM, a Protestant, residing in Killconnell, parish of
Killmaccrenan, County Donegal, 1654. [CS]; there in 1659.
[C]

WALKER, GEORGE, clerk, Justice of the Peace for County
Antrim, 1675. [NAS.RH9.17.103]

WALKER, HARRY, servant to Patrick Hanney in Wigtonshire,
alleged armed assault, fled to Ireland in September 1630.
[RPCS.IV.94]

WALKER, JEAN. Process of Adherence, James Wardel, servant to
John Devon in Easton, against Jean Walker in Ireland, his
spouse, married at West Calder in February 1668.
[NAS.CC8.Consistorial Processes, 1680]

WALKER, JOHN, a Protestant and leasee in the parish of Rapho,
County Donegal, 1654. [CS]

WALLACE, DAVID, in the Barony of Glenarm, 1650s.
[NAS.GD154.512]

WALLACE, JANET, spouse of John Wallace a workman in
Ireland, 1621. [NAS.RS.Ayr#2/155]

WALLACE, ROBERT, in the Barony of Glenarm, 1650s.
[NAS.GD154.512]

WALLACE, THOMAS, a gentleman in the parish of
Clandevadocke, Barony of Killmccrenan, County Donegal,
1659. [C]

WALLACE, ..., in the Barony of Antrim, 1659. [C]

WALLIS, Lieutenant Colonel JAMES, in the Barony of Belfast, County Antrim, 1659. [C]

WARK, JOHN, 1673. [NAS.RH15.91.60]

WARNOCK, ROBERT, born around 1665, moved to Ireland in 1679, returned and settled in Thornton, parish of Kilbryde, by 1685. [RPCS.XI.264]

WATSON, WILLIAM, in Ireland, 1643. [NAS.GD150/3520/10]

WATSON, WILLIAM, a minister residing in the Glebe lands of the parish of Enver, County Donegal, 1654. [CS]

WAUGH, GEORGE, a Presbyterian minister in northern Ireland, 1679. [RPCS.VI.657]

WAUGH, JOHN, 1694. [NAS.RH15.91.60]

WEIR, JOHN, (1), in the Barony of Glenarm, 1650s. [NAS.GD154.512]

WEIR, JOHN, (2), in the Barony of Glenarm, 1650s. [NAS.GD154.512]

WEIR, WILLIAM, moved from Ayr to Ireland before 1681. [Ayr Burgh Accounts, 18 April 1681]

WELSH, the widow, 1694. [NAS.RH15.91.60]

WHARRY, JAMES, born 1691, died 16 September 1757. [Carncastle g/s, County Antrim]

WHITE, HUGH, in the Barony of Glenarm, 1650s. [NAS.GD154.512]

WHITE, ISABELLA, born 1702, wife of James Blackwood in Bangor, died 5 June 1729. [Bangor Old Abbey g/s]

WHITE, JOHN, in the Barony of Glenarm, 1650s. [NAS.GD154.512]

WHITE, THOMAS, tenant of 45 acres in the parish of Kilwaghter, 1690, 1691, 1692. [NAS.GD154.525/527/528/530]

WHYT, HEW, a merchant burgess of Irvine, Ayrshire, only son of the late Steven Whyt a former provost of Irvine, was about to move to Ireland on 8 August 1662. [Irvine Burgh Records]

WHYTE, ADAM, minister in Dunluce, County Antrim, a deed in favour of his son George Whyte in the lands of Murthogall in the parish of Lesmahagow, Lanarkshire, 29 May 1699. [NAS.GD1.179.51]

WILKINS, JAMES, in the Barony of Glenarm, 1650s. [NAS.GD154.512]

WILLCOCKS, ISACHER, a merchant in Dublin, was admitted as a burgess and guildsbrother of Glasgow on 13 January 1724. [BRG]

WILLIAMSON, DAVID, in Killyleagh, County Down, 1671. [NAS.RH15.91.62]

WILIAMSON, Captain DAVID, 1674. [NAS.RH15.91.60]

WILLIAMSON, JAMES, a merchant, 1694. [NAS.RH15.91.60]

WILLIAMSON, PHILIP, master of the James of Donaghadie at Kirkcudbright on 8 September 1673. [NAS.E72.6.2]

WILSON, HUGH, a Presbyterian minister in northern Ireland, 1679. [RPCS.VI.657]

WILSON, HUGH, a merchant in Belfast, was admitted as a burgess and guilds-brother of Ayr on 21 August 1722. [ABR]

WILSON, JAMES, a merchant in Butcher's gate, Londonderry, 1659. [C]

WILSON, JAMES, a tenant in parish of Kilwaghter, 1690/ 1691. [NAS.GD154.526/1, 2]

WILSON, JANET, in the Barony of Glenarm, 1650s. [NAS.GD154.512]

WILSON, JOHN, fisher in Glasgow, was alleged to have supplied weapons to the rebels in Ireland, 1601. [RPCS.V.324]

WILSON, JOHN, in the Barony of Glenarm, 1650s, tenant of 4 acres in the parish of Kilwaghter, 1660s. [NAS.GD154.512/525]

WILSON, LANCELOT, a merchant in Belfast, was admitted as a burgess and guilds-brother of Ayr on 29 June 1719. [ABR]

WILSON, ROBERT, a merchant in Belfast, was admitted as a burgess and guilds-brother of Ayr on 13 August 1713. [ABR]

WILSON, ROBERT, in Kilwaghter, 1690. [NAS.GD154.527/1]

WILSON, THOMAS, 1673. [NAS.RH15.91.60]

WILSON, WILLIAM, a traveller in Ireland, 1601. [Irvine Burgh Accounts, 1601]

WILSON, WILLIAM, was granted part of Aghagalla in the precinct of Liffer, Barony of Rapho, County Donegal, 1611. [TCD]

WILSON, WILLIAM, 1694. [NAS.RH15.91.60]

WILSON, WILLIAM, a merchant in Belfast, was admitted as a burgess and guilds-brother of Ayr on 24 February 1713. [ABR]

WILSON, ..., in the Barony of Massareene, County Antrim, 1659. [C]

WINTER, KATE, a kitchen-servant, 1668. [NAS.RH15.91.60]

WOODS, MICHAEL, sr., yeoman of the Falls, Belfast, 1678. [NAS.GD10.823]

WOODS, NICOLAS, from County Down, a soldier, to return from Scotland to Ireland in 1689. [RPCS.XIII.425]

WOODS, RICHARD, 1674. [NAS.RH15.91.60]

WOODSIDE, ROBERT, in the Barony of Glenarm, 1650s.
[NAS.GD154.512]

WRIGHT, HUGH, in the Barony of Glenarm, 1650s.
[NAS.GD154.512]

WRIGHT, WILLIAM, in the Barony of Glenarm, 1650s.
[NAS.GD154.512]

WYLLIE, ADAM, tenant of 38 acres in Lelis in the parish of
Kilwaghter, 1690, 1692, 1695.
[NAS.GD154.525/527/530/532]

WYLLIE, CATHERINE, only daughter of the late Robert Wyllie
in Karnecassill, County Antrim, wife of Robert Reid in
Mayokill, County Londonderry, heir to uncle Hugh Wyllie
son of the late John Wyllie at the Mill of Ardrossan, Ayrshire,
5 February 1661. [NAS.GD1.693.6]

WYLLIE, HUGH, in the Barony of Glenarm, 1650s.
[NAS.GD154.512]

WYLLIE, JAMES, tenant of 15 acres in the Barony of Glenarm,
1650s. [NAS.GD154.512/515]

WYLLIE, JOHN, a Protestant and leasee in the parish of Rapho,
County Donegal, 1654. [CS]

WYLLIE, JOHN, tenant of 14 acres in Drumedonachie, 1695.
[NAS.GD154.532]

WYLLIE, JOHN, 1694. [NAS.RH15.91.60]

WYLLIE, JOHN, a merchant in Belfast, was admitted as a burgess
and guilds-brother of Ayr on 9 April 1718. [ABR]

WYLLIE, MATTHEW, 1694. [NAS.RH15.91.60]

WYLLIE, THOMAS, a minister at Coleraine, 1672.
[NAS.CH1/5/6/128-143]

WYLLIE, WILLIAM, tenant of 38 acres in Mickel Well, Lelish,
parish of Kilwaghter, 1690, 1691. [NAS.GD154.525/528]

WYLLIE, WILLIAM, born 1705, died 24 February 1777. [Carncastle g/s, County Antrim]

YOUNG, ARCHIBALD, a Presbyterian minister in northern Ireland, 1679. [RPCS.VI.657]

YOUNG, Sir JAMES, an undertaker in County Longford, 1621. [RPCS.XII.420]

YOUNG, JAMES, in Lilbane, 1725. [NAS.GD10.454]

YOUNG, JOHN, a tenant in Drumnicho, in May 1645. [NAS.GD154.509]

YOUNG, JOHN, a gentleman in Tolyosaran, County Armagh, 1659. [C]

YOUNG, JOHN, in Castbine, 1721. [NAS.GD10.450]

YOUNG, MARGARET, born 1672, wife of Robert Tweed, died 11 January 1740. [Carncastle g/s, County Antrim]

YOUNG, ROBERT, in Culdrum, parish of Taboyne, County Donegal, 1654. [CS]

YOUNG, ROBERT, in the Barony of Glenarm, 1650s. [NAS.GD154.512]

YOUNG, ROBERT, in Belfast, 1685. [NAS.GD10.832]

YOUNG, WILLIAM, son of the late Robert Young a merchant in Antrim, 1650. [NAS.CC8.8.65/165]

YOUNG, WILLIAM, a gentleman in Drumban, parish of Donoghmore, Barony of Rapho, County Donegal, 1659. [C]

..........., husband of Kathleen Hamilton, moved from Arran, Scotland, to Ireland around 1637. [RSA#2/20]

REFERENCES

ARCHIVES

NAS = National Archives of Scotland, Edinburgh

NLI = National Library of Ireland, Dublin

PUBLICATIONS

BRG = Burgess Roll of Glasgow

BSD = Books of Survey and Distribution, 1636-1703,
[Dublin, 1949]

C = Census of Ireland, circa 1659. [Dublin, 1939]

CBP = Calendar of Borders Papers, [Edinburgh, 1896]

CS = Civil Survey of Donegal, Londonderry and Tyrone,
[Dublin, 1937]

CSPS = Calendar of State Papers, Scotland

DFI = Danish Force in Ireland, [Dublin, 1962]

GBR = Extracts from the Records of the Burgh of Glasgow,
[Glasgow, 1905]

KSR = Kirk Session Records

MM = Montgomery's Manuscripts, [G. Hill]

RPCS= Register of the Privy Council of Scotland, series

RSA = Records of the Synod of Argyll, 1639-1662, [Edinburgh

TCD = Trinity College, Dublin, ms N.2.2